J. Samuel Williams, Jr.

Exilic Existence

Contributions of Black Churches in Prince Edward County, Virginia During the Modern Civil Rights Movement

Exilic Existence

Exilic Existence

Contributions of Black Churches in Prince Edward County,
Virginia During the Modern Civil Rights Movement

J. Samuel Williams, Jr.

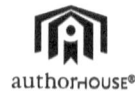

authorHOUSE®

AuthorHouse™
1663 Liberty Drive
Bloomington, IN 47403
www.authorhouse.com
Phone: 1-800-839-8640

First published by AuthorHouse   10/13/2011

ISBN: 978-1-4670-3696-2 (sc)
ISBN: 978-1-4670-3695-5 (ebk)

Library of Congress Control Number: 2011916789

Printed in the United States of America

Dedicated to our Grandchildren

Each of whom is pictured on the front cover taken October, 2006 in front of The First Baptist Church

Isaac Dauda, III—"Cairo"

James Samuel Williams—"Bee-Nee"

Ann-Marie—"Bunchie"

Marvin L.—"Trey"

Abena Ann—"Ab"

Hopefully, they will prove to the world that "the pen is mightier than the sword."

In Memory

of my Maternal Grandmother

Lena Scott Johnson (1888-1951)

She taught me how to write years prior to elementary school. She possessed an unusually beautiful penmanship, would often cease writing and say, "Listen, here boy, when they said: 'Let's write,' I was there."

Toward the Memory of my Parents

James Samuel Williams, Senior 1913-2010

A native of Hampden-Sydney, Virginia and through his Journeyman's trade; taught me the skill of preciseness and the ethics of Grace through individual trials and collective tribulations!

Nannie Johnson Williams Butler, 1909-1958

She was a rural elementary school principal in adjoining Cumberland County's "Cotton-town" section in the school established by Robert Russa Moton (1867-1940).

Moton's earliest teaching and educational organizing skills were begun while a student at Hampton Institute (University as of 1984). The school bore his name until it was demolished in the late 1970's or early 1980's.

Mama Nannie was my "built-in, home bound" elementary school instructor. And, upon the absence of my fifth grade teacher due to illness, my mother stood in her stead as my second semester teacher.

Professional Biography
of
J. Samuel Williams, Jr.

A native New Yorker, J. Samuel Williams, Jr. completed his elementary and high school education in Farmville, Virginia, located in the County of Prince Edward.

He received a Bachelor of Arts Degree from the Shaw University in Raleigh, North Carolina and a Master of Divinity Degree from the School of Theology, Virginia Union University in Richmond, Virginia.

Mr. Williams began to display early signs of leadership during the 1951 student strike at the Robert R. Moton High School in Farmville. This case, in addition to four other locations in this nation, was used as a "test case" which provided the impetus and foundation for the historic 1954 Supreme Court decision regarding education.

His interest in civil and human rights was continued as he actively participated in protest demonstrations in Raleigh, North Carolina and Prince Edward County during the 1960's at which time he and others were jailed for such actions. During his matriculation at Shaw, he assisted in the founding of the Student Non-Violent Coordinating Committee (SNCC) with Dr. Martin Luther King, Jr. and his staff in 1960. Having worked in the former Federal Office of Economic Opportunity (OEO) under the Lyndon Johnson Administration, his social concerns were extended to that of Head Start teacher, Deputy Service to America (VISTA) in Buffalo, New York and Planner for the Central Piedmont Department of Religious Studies at the State University of New York at Buffalo and Executive Director of the Department of Social Service for the Council of Churches.

Mr. Williams has published articles in several periodicals: among these has been a weekly column in the former Richmond

Afro-American newspaper under the title, "The Black Church Speaks."

Among his educational and missionary tours, he has traveled to Korea, Japan, Greece, Egypt, Canada, Guyana, South America; Jamaica, West Indies and Italy.

The Ecumenical Service Award presented by the Catholic Dioceses of Western New York; and having been elected to Who's Who in Religion in America are among his many accolades. The Virginia University (formerly Virginia Seminary and College) of Lynchburg, Virginia presented him with a plaque for his outstanding Deanship in the School of Religion, and he was elected to Men of Distinction in Oxford, England.

He has pastored five churches including the historic First Baptist Church of Farmville, from which the 1954 Supreme Court Decision was partly launched. Presently, he is minister of the Levi Baptist Church in Prince Edward County, to which he was recalled in 1997 after twenty-nine years of absence.

Mr. Williams was also a founding board member of the Robert R. Moton Museum, Inc. and has worked with the office of Multicultural Affairs at Longwood University for over eight years. Some of the activities in which he participated include: being the keynote speaker for the Martin Luther King, Jr. program, African American History month program, and at Longwood's Citizen Leader Day and Kwanzaa presenter for the Festival of Lights programs.

Mr. Williams is married to the former Lyllie A. Blanton of Farmville, Virginia and they are the blessed parents of three productive daughters and the grandparents of five aspiring grandchildren.

Of Gratitude, In Depth

(Acknowledgements)

After having traversed this work through the corridors of my consciousness for at least two decades, my debt is monumental and enormous.

Foremost, my deepest debt is to Our Father, the Deliverer; His Son Jesus, the Liberator; and the Holy Ghost as Comforter and Guide!

My wife, Ann, our children: Jamantha Agape, Psyche Aletheia and Omega Athenia, have provided the much needed intellectual exposure through their academics and diverse learning life styles. Their husbands are commended for continued inspirations and through the use of their homes in burning the "all night oil". They are: Isaac Dauda, Akai Kwame, and Marvin Lee; Watson, Forson and Wilson, respectively. **Note**: The original manuscript was typed by one who volunteered without asking, our daughter, Jamantha.

Patrice Carter, Program Coordinator of The Robert Russa Moton Museum, was the "tug boat typist" who first pulled the boat out from the harbor, so that Jamantha and Andrea Bridge might set sail.

Encouragement through my pastor, James P. Ashton and his family; Reverends, Wyatt Tee Walker, Ralph Reavis and Percy L. High were much needed at all points along this work's development.

Imperative research at the following institutions was conducted at: Shaw University; Virginia Union University; Longwood University; and the Robert Russa Moton Museum: A Study in Civil Rights Education.

Dr. Larissa S. Ferguson, of Longwood University, provided lecture time for her classes and during summer months to teachers and students from William and Mary College, the University of Virginia and various High Schools throughout the state at the Moton Museum. Outside of these areas her motivation has always been much needed and right on time. Also of Longwood, Mark Lenker, the library's Assistant Instruction/Reference Services Librarian, has occupied a "can't do without" position in the area of massive computerization utilization regarding this work and my planning trips to: Guyana, South America; Jamaica, West Indies; and cities throughout Italy.

Numerous friends, street folk and others have been guiding lights along this literary journey. Church Pastors and clerks have been of powerful assistance. Reverend William Thompson, former campus Minister at Hampden-Sydney's University Church for providing written materials. Interviews with Dr. Ronald Heinemann of Hampden-Sydney College; Edwilda Allen of The Martha E. Forrester Council of Women; Robert Hamlin of The Nation of Islam; Joseph Williams of the Baha'i Faith, the Secretaries of the Unitarian Universalists Church of Richmond, Virginia; and Leeman Allen of Calvary Baptist Church in Prospect for information regarding The True Reformers.

Additional gratitude goes to the following people:

To Edward H. Peeples, Ph.D. for such a groundbreaking interview in his Richmond residence. His final words to me upon my departure were: "Sam, this is a powerful and extensive undertaking, I just hope you will live long enough to see it completed." Both he and Ruby Clayton of Richmond, Virginia conducted a much revealed and needed study in the county during the sizzlin' 6o's.

For Mary "Vickie" Morton who shared information regarding The Hampden-Sydney Benevolent and Beneficial Society, topped off with a scrumptious supper based on her experience as a caterer extraordinaire!

Frances Goldman Scott, a native of Hampden-Sydney, for recommending sound resources in that locale. Goldman was also a former high school class mate at "Old, Ole Moton," as to which we so frequently referred.

In deep appreciation to Dwana Waugh, a Graduate Research Assistant and Doctoral candidate at the University of North Carolina in chapel Hill. Dialoging with her concerning the 1951 Student Strike and the 1959-1964 closing of public schools by an all white racists Board of County Supervisors, she exclaimed: "What actually happened was this, you [Student Strikers] did something to them and they did something to you!" After she spoke, I immediately thought of a hit by James Brown, cut in 1973: "Revenge! 'The Big Payback.'"

Certainly, not among the least of these is Andrea L. Bridge, who's typing of the manuscripts; adding, deleting, rearranging sentence structures and making suggestions became mandatory. Deep and indelible gratitude is also due her for being my copy editor, and to The Farmville-Prince Edward County Library.

PART I

Early Christian, Philanthropic, and Humanitarian Zeal
that Pioneered the Modern Civil Rights Movement,
1848-1920

Write the Vision;

Make it plain on tablets,

so that a runner may read it.

For there is still a vision for the appointed time;

it speaks of the end and does not lie.

If it seems to tarry, wait for it,

it will surely come,

it will not delay.

Habakkuk 2:2B-3

NRSV

Part I

Early Christian, Philanthropic, and Humanitarian Zeal that Pioneered the Modern Civil Rights Movement, 1848-1920

Part II

The Magnetization of Black Churches Relative to Interfaith Action and Response

Forward[1]

More often than not, the truth about African Americans has not been accurately told about our smaller communities. In times past and sometimes today; what we have been told is that anything done by black people had little if any worth. However, James Samuel Williams, Jr. has elevated the contributions and achievements of African Americans in Prince Edward County. He has done this by summoning the cannons of historical research and shot through the canvas of historical records smeared with paint full of falsehoods. Now, the Black and White citizens of Prince Edward County can see and appreciate the achievements of African Americans in and to society. Brother Williams has demonstrated that, who we are and what we have done is worth mentioning. What he has done is to reverse the written records of Western Civilization. Therefore, his work is corrective as well as informational. The inclusion of our records had to be done by an African American who lived as witness and participant. His work will fill the gap in the historical account of African Americans of Prince Edward County; especially the clergy, the teachers, and the ordinary citizens who now sleep beneath the sacred sod upon which they trod. Williams has applied the **light of truth** to the darkness of the hidden and forgotten and now we can see more clearly. James S. Williams' thorough research has slain the dragons of western civilizations' suppression of Black truth; thereby putting everything out in the open and little if any is hidden.

I would highly recommend his book to be put upon the shelves of all Universities and Colleges, Clergy, Churches, Citizens, Educators, and all as a **sterling example** of what should be replicated in other communities across America. The African American Church in particular and the people in Prince Edward County in general and beyond are indebted to J.S. Williams, Jr. for his fine work.

---

[1] Source: Ralph Reavis—President and sometimes frumentious Professor, PhD. of Ecclesiastical History and Global Missions, Seminary Hill, Lynchburg, Virginia

Introduction

The insatiable appetite of the media, both print and television to fix personalities to radical movements that alter in revolutionary terms, the sociology of the nation particularly in matters of race and ethnicity, they often create a void of the institutions that produce those individuals. So it is with African American Church. In the larger picture, had there been no African American Church, there would have been no Movement! Sam Williams has filled that void in this work. The Brown vs. the Board of Education Supreme Court decision undid the decades of evil done by the Plessy vs. Ferguson decision of the previous century. It killed the "separate but equal practice" of southern politicians. It promised a new day of hopes and aspirations of African Americans unlike any legislation before or after.

The African American Church is the unsung hero of Black progress in America. Sam Williams has corrected this deficiency in a well documented way and at the same time given credence to its partners that it produced along the way of its tedious journey. Close and careful scrutiny will reveal again and again that the African American Church remains the institution of primary influence in Black life and community; the African American Church is the Black community! Nothing claims the loyalty or investment of finance as the African American Church. It is the largest business in Black life, the center of sociality, the cultural reservoir of Black life, the origin of all protests for freedom and justice. There would be no NAACP if there were no African American Church. It permeates all of Black life, sacred and secular.

The intrinsic value of Sam Williams' work is to open a new discussion as to how institutions affect sociological change through the personalities that it shapes and produces. If there had not been an African American Church there would be no Martin Luther

King, Jr., et al. The Movement was a church movement, through and through. Most of the so-called "King scholars" have ignored the influence of the Church's impact on the shaping the construct of his life. They have tried to make it something else;—namely Gandhi, Boston University, et al.

Serious and diligent research will reveal that the molding influence overwhelmingly has been the influence of the African American Church in the life of this gargantuan world figure, Martin Luther King, Jr.!!!

Though Williams' book is localized in the Prince Edward instance which admittedly had far-reaching national importance, it is in microcosm a general defect of "historical reporting and analysis."[2]

---

[2]   Source: Wyatt Tee Walker: Theologian, Author, Cultural Historian, and former Chief of Staff to Martin Luther King, Jr.

Concerning My Labors Herein

Much has been written, taught and lectured upon regarding Brown versus Board of Education, the 1954 Supreme Court Decision, and the School Closing years of 1959-1964 in the County of Prince Edward.

The historical, psychological, sociological, political and other unnamed areas have been expounded upon in the above areas, but nothing has been written relative to the toils and labors of the Black Church's contributions. I have identified a sweltering void, an abyss, in this particular area and it is here I intend to open closed eyes.

Firstly, the work consists of three individual but related occurrences from the perspectives of racial equality and social justice. Part One, the reader will observe, elevated early movements in the county that ploughed, unbeknownst to them, rich raw material needed to set in motion positive protests. Every movement for the betterment of a "**cause**" has its antecedents. Here we identify:

1. Hampden-Sydney Beneficial and Benevolent Society
2. The First Baptist Church
3. The Grand United Fountain of the Order of the True Reformers, and
4. The Martha E. Forrester Council of Colored Women.

Secondly, the Student-led Strike which occurred on April 23, 1951, was one of the five "Test Cases" used in Prince Edward County Brown versus Board of Education.

Thirdly, the School Closings 1959-1964, with connections of street protests and demonstrations assisted in the desegregation of public facilities

The reader should be aware of two prominent trains of thought:

1. The term "Black Church" is not relegated to this ethnicity per se. In some instances the term does stand alone; in others it invokes the presence of interracial and interdenominational constituencies'.
2. The reader should not become disappointed, dismayed or discouraged if certain areas are sparsely touched upon or not mentioned at all.

This is true because the author's primary prerogative is that of the illumination of spiritual and religious contributions within the context of the churches who responded to the Trumpeter's call of social justice and human equality! Throughout the sizzlin' 60's the Civil Rights Movement became known as **A Moral Issue,** thus indicative of spiritual and religious significance.

Finally, the more one writes, one soon discovers that there is much more in need of being written. I mentioned this to Ronald Heinemann, Professor emeritus at Hampden-Sydney College in a September 9, 2009 interview. He smiled and responded: "True, you must have a cut-off point." Somewhere I read where Alice Walker, authoress of: "*The Color Purple* "stated: "Writing is a mystical experience."

These two thoughts were among those that were paramount in the penning of this twenty year undertaking. They presented the greatest of all challenges. A "cut-off point" means one cannot divert, transfer or modify any longer. A "mystical experience" connotes writing non-stop or intermittingly, when the Spirit speaks!

Prologue

Racial Uplift and the Investment of the Black Church

The concept of racial uplift and self-determination within the Church has always dominated Black social, political and economic thought. It has been a broad concept, adapted by many denominations; that covered issues such as equal rights, moral, spiritual, and intellectual development as well as institutional and organizational practices. The rhetoric of racial uplift and self-determination has helped to create many Black leaders within the churches, schools, communities; the national and even at the global level. For example, this idealistic perspective can be seen in the limited but frugal manner in which the people participated. For the Church, even the sacrifice of funds for the sake of equality, educational attainment and ultimately racial uplift was a target area as the church sought to embrace a commitment with this outcome. Motivated to give, many would not in their lifetime see the fruits of their financial investments but believed that through the Church they would be contributors in the project of racial uplift and self-determination. Ultimately, the move toward the greater good was what was valued beyond anything else. Even today, the literature of the Black church is focused on the need for alternative methods of a continuing struggle of uplift and movement toward increasing progress.[3]

---

[3]   This Prologue was contributed by Deneese L. Jones, Ph.D.; Dean, College of Education and Human Services at Longwood University.

The County: Prince Edward—Its Founding, 1754

The County Seat-Farmville—Its Formation, 1778

Adopting its name from Prince Edward Augustus (1739-1767), a son of Frederick, Prince of Wales, United Kingdom of England, the county is located practically in the state of Virginia's center. Obviously this position renders itself to brief time travel throughout the state utilizing Routes 15 North and South, 460 and 360 East and West and connecting with other State Routes within a fifty-mile radius, yielding to major Interstate Highways.

In terms of geographical dimensions, the county is 357 (917km²), square miles measuring approximately 25x25 miles in terms of length and breadth. The overwhelming majority of this strip of terrain encompasses rural territory, which has proven to be great grounds for almost all kinds of outdoor delights and diversified agriculture.

Breached from the adjoining county of Amelia in the aforementioned year, the U.S. Census of 2000 recorded a population of 19,720 persons. For Farmville proper the population of 6,845 is hereby included. A breakdown of the town population encompassed an enrollment of students at Longwood College (University as of 2002), and for the county, an enrollment of students enrolled at Hampden-Sydney College in Hampden-Sydney, Virginia.

These two institutions of higher education have always claimed the county as "home": Longwood University founded in 1839 as the Female Seminary for Women and Hampden-Sydney College founded in 1775. According to their records, both graduated their first Black students in 1972. "University" status was granted to Longwood under the social, intellectual, and keen insightful leadership of Patricia Picard Cormier, Ph.D., a powerful "people's person," a friendly title I draped upon her on our first encounter, the day of her inauguration in 1997.

The village and college of Hampden-Sydney is named after John Hampden (1594-1643), and Algernon Sydney (1662-1683), both outstanding Englishmen.

It should be of interest to note that the college is one of three all male liberal arts "mainstream" colleges in the Nation. In the order of their founding, they are:

1.) Hampden-Sydney-1775

2). Wabash College-1832

3). Morehouse College-1867; an all Black Institution with its beginnings in Augusta, Georgia.

Commencing with the September, 2009 academic year, Christopher B. Howard, Ph.D., began his fundraising, intellectual and scholastic labors as Hampden-Sydney's first Black president. Attending his inauguration on November 11, 2010 brought dynamic elation to my mind! What an exhilarating experience!

His undergraduate achievements were completed at the Air Force Academy, a Master's received in Business Administration from Harvard and a Ph.D. from Oxford University, England, a Rhodes Scholar; if you please!

Dr. Howard's zealously contributing and friendly family, in whose presence I have been delightfully graced on numerous occasions, are Barbara, a brilliant and beautiful Johannesburg, South African sister who pulls poise and grace in her train; and their two studious sons: Cohen and Joshua, high school matriculates. Praise DE LAWD on Earth and Glory to GAWD in Zion!

Farmville, an embryonic epicenter of sorts, serves as axis for seven encircling counties in Central Virginia. The almost incredible and phenomenal growth, since the 1970's, has been magnetized to this town; for instance, the rapid state of the art expansion, health facilities, cultural expressions, hotel accommodations, education enrichments, and shopping plazas. The Civil Rights Heritage Trail (begun 2007), commencing at the Robert Russa Moton Museum (formally the Robert Russa Moton High School from which the student—led strike was launched April23, 1951); and numerous other areas of inquiry. Note: the latter part of The Heritage Trail presently consists of forty-one sights, including six in Farmville.

It is here that the famed Heart of Virginia Festival is conducted annually on the first weekend in the month of May. It was begun in 1979 under the skilled and cooperating leadership of Town Manager, Gerald Spates, another "people's person." This is often facetiously referred to as "Gerald's Day!" From the state's capital, Farmville is located in a sixty mile southwesterly direction. Lynchburg is located fifty miles in a Northwesterly direction. Thus, the three locations form a triangular area.

As silently as it is maintained, the county is situated in that which is known as **"The Black Belt."** Such a name had its origination during slavery. This **"Belt"** traverses its way from Delaware through Eastern Texas and Northern Mississippi. In his illuminating autobiography entitled: *Up From Slavery;* Booker Taliaferro Washington (1895-1915), a native Virginian from Hales Ford, describes this area as follows: "The term [Black Belt] was first used to designate a part of the country possessing this thick dark and naturally rich soil was of course that part of the south where the slaves were the most profitable and consequently were taken in large numbers. Later, and especially since the war, the term seems to be used wholly in a political sense—that is to designate the counties where Black people outnumbered the whites." Washington's counterpart, William Edward Burghardt DuBois Ph.D. (1868-1963), wrote in that superlative intellectually inspiring discourse: *The Souls of Black Folk,* concerning this subject as related to the state of Georgia: "How curious a land is this—how full of untold story, a tragedy and a laughter, and the rich legacy of human life; shadowed with a tragic past and big with future promise. This is the Black Belt of Georgia. It is a land of rapid contrasts and curiously mingled hope and pain."

Parenthetically, while passing through, it is significant to know that Washington and DuBois viewed educational achievements from two different perspectives for Black people. For Washington, vocational and industrial education were stressed; for DuBois, a high intellectual liberal arts stance was taken.

Having succeeded Washington as second principal (president), of Tuskegee Institute (University as of 1985), Robert Russa Moton (1867-1940) served as mediator and brought a profound balance between these two ideological extremities. Moton was a native of Virginia (Amelia County), but at an early age relocated to Prince Edward County where he attended public school. His place of abode still stands stately in the "Rice" hamlet of the county.

Possessed at least by a dual definition amid others, the **Black Belt** (soil and race) became the land through which the majority of the racial revolutions throughout the southern tier have been waged. Therefore, in its quarter moon shape, I have termed it:

FREEDOM'S FERTILE CRESCENT!

Upon the soil, the final stages of the Civil War (1861-1865) were fought. Through John Brown's (1800-1859) creative abolitionist's efforts, this war was begun at Harper's Ferry, Virginia. It became a part of West Virginia in 1863. Of Brown, Vernon N. Johns (1892-1965), said to me while chauffeuring him up and down the East coast, "He made the war that made us free."

Like the adjoining county of Buckingham, Prince Edward has had numerous native Black sons and daughters who have contributed immensely toward the triumph of Black people. Some of its contributors who are classified in this category are:

Native Sons

Tazewell Branch (1828-1925) was a Member of The House of Delegates. He purchased land in 1868-1869 for Beulah African Methodist Episcopal Church. He worked for the Thackston family as servant, and as a shoemaker. He is buried in the Odd Fellows Cemetery in Farmville.[4]

James W. D. Bland (1844-1927) was a Member of the Virginia State Senate, a representative of the counties of Appomattox and Prince Edward. His death came as a result of the collapsing of a floor in the Supreme Court Building in the State Capital on April 27, 1870. He is interred in Odd Fellows Cemetery in Farmville.

Blanche Kelso Bruce (1841-1898), Bruce was born in the far eastern part of Prince Edward County in the hamlet of Green Bay. I was sent to pastor the Levi Baptist Church in this village from January 1962 to June 1968; following a journey of pastoring, working in "Specialized Social Ministries" in Buffalo, New York and for the Office of Economic Opportunity. I was recalled to this pastorate in 1997, and have remained there since. A state marker was erected to honor the memory of Senator Bruce on the west side of Route 360 in the hamlet of Green Bay.

"The only Negro ever to serve in the United States Senate was born in slavery on a Prince Edward farm. Blanche Kelso Bruce was taught to read and write by his master's son. He was educated at Oberlin College and after the war, between the states settled in Mississippi. He was elected to the United States Senate from Mississippi. He served one term, 1875-1881. Subsequently, he was Register in the Treasury 1881-1891, and 1897-1898."[5]

Nathaniel M Griggs—represented the county in the House of Delegates during the years of 1883-1884, and the Senate from 1887-1890.

William D. Evans—was a member of the House of Delegates from 1877-1880); he was a Constable, a contractor and an overseer of roads.

Alexander Bigger—Bigger, a creative and inventive genius with a memory of "total recall," invented the mechanism, a railroad track switch, which lowered and elevated gates at railroad

---

[4]   Note: "Odd Fellows" is the name of a Fraternal Order, having nothing in common with a person's character or behavioral pattern.

[5]   Source: *History of Prince Edward County, Virginia: From Its Earliest Settlements through Its Establishment in 1754 to Its Bicentennial Year,* by Clarence Herbert Bradshaw

crossings. Prior to this invention, gates were set in motion from a tower operated manually by a "watchman."

With the elimination of this employee, the engine now trips the switch and lowers the gates, the last railroad car trips the switch and the gates return to their vertical position.

Before he could obtain a patent for it, the idea in print was stolen. At the time of his death during the latter 1940's, he was working on another invention, in secluded secrecy. I shared elementary school classrooms with his youngest grandchildren: Alexander and Virginia. Also, Virginia and I were high school classmates.

Information of this invention was first brought to our attention by Reverend Arthur E. Jordan (see below). Brother Bigger is buried in the cemetery of the New Witt Baptist Church in the county.[6]

Arthur Edward Jordan (1893-1959). He was a pastor, High School Principal, my sixth grade Teacher and Athletic Coach. Jordan was graduated from Virginia Seminary and College, a tremendously inspiring influence on High and Elementary school students.

In Grade Six, each day began with singing Negro Spirituals as "Morning devotions." Black History was taught directly or in passing reference to White or European occurrences. Reverend Jordan was the first person to introduce us to the positive accomplishing side of Black People.

James "Pee Wee" Jenkins (1923-2002). A native of Hampden-Sydney, Jenkins played professional baseball with the Negro National League.

He was a refined and polished pitcher who blazed a trail in the following teams: the Cincinnati—Indianapolis Clowns, 1944-1955; the New York Cubans, 1946-1950; the Birmingham Black Barons, 1944—and the Canadian League, 1952. Upon lecturing at Hampden-Sydney College in the late 90's, I recall him having said: "how nervous and thrilled I was when I first pitched in Yankee Stadium."

The Negro National League was begun by baseball's super genius, Andrew "Rube" Foster (1879-1930). Through his ingenuity and prayerful maturation, there were a total of twenty-four teams

---

6   Source: Magnolia B. Hayes, Granddaughter.

comprising the League. Because of wide-spread mass based segregation and discrimination and all of their tentacles; these superb teams have basically become unknown.

Traveling intra and interstate by buses, many in need of constant repairs, it was counted as a good days work for teams to play a "triple header" from sun up to sun down! What dogged determination and strength of Black Soul Power did this reveal!

Jenkins had established a brotherly friendship with Black players in the recognized leagues because they too had played previously with the National Negro Leagues prior to entering America's major league teams. Such characters were: Joe Black, 1924-2002; Roy Campanella, 1921-1993; Don Newcombe, 1926—; Leroy Robert "Satchel" Paige, 1906-1982; Jackie Roosevelt Robinson, 1919-1972; and a much larger number dispersed throughout the majors.

Native Daughters

Mary Elizabeth Branch (1881-1944). She became the first woman President of Tillotson College, in Austin, Texas from 1930-1944. Affiliates of the college are the United Methodist Church, United church of Christ and the United Negro College Fund (UNCF).

The name of the former Robert Russa Moton Elementary School where I attended was changed to The Mary Elizabeth

Branch Elementary School in 1964. It is presently, The Farmville Recreation Center. Mary Elizabeth Branch was the daughter of previously mentioned House of Delegates Member, Tazewell Branch.

Mozella Jordan Price (b.?-1971). A native of Prince Edward County and sister of my sixth grade teacher, Arthur Edward Jordan, she became Supervisor of Schools in adjoining Appomattox County from 1919-1963.

In that county she established Camp Winona a huge house with lake and other forms of recreation. Our seventh grade class experienced the joys of picnicking there in 1946. The facility was used as a school for boys and girls. It still remains on the east bound lane of State Route 460. Sister Price matriculated at Boydton Institute, Hampton Institute (University as of 1984), and Columbia University.

Carver-Price High School in Appomattox County was named in her honor as well as George Washington Carver (1865?-1943). Her brother Arthur served as Principal at this historic academic facility. She was an Educator, Lecturer and daughter of Reverend Nelson Jordan, and wife of Reverend Peter Price, who died in 1944.

Of Our Striven and Striving Sisters

Women and minorities should become first line soldiers. It's time to work together to ensure full participation of women here at home. I'm proud to come from a long line of women who are not afraid to shake things up.[7]

Economics is the study of who gets what, when, where and why. It is the study of the way factors of production; land, labor, capital and creativity are paid in rent, wages, interest and profits. It is the history of the knife, of how the pie is sliced. And it is the story of why African Americans get so much less of our fair share of the pie[8].

---

[7]   Donna Lease Brazille (1959-) Authoress, Professor, Political Analyst and Chairwoman of Albert Gores' Presidential Campaign

[8]   Julianne Marie Malveaux, Ph.D-(1953-) President of Bennett College, Economist and Authoress

I can't read, but I can hear. I have heard the Bible and have learned that Eve caused man to sin. Well, if woman upset the world, give her a chance to set it right side up again[9].

Women, if the soul of a nation is to be saved, I believe that you must become its soul.[10]

I had to fight for what I achieved no matter what accomplishments you make, somebody helped you.[11]

My administration shall thus endeavor to give Liberian women prominence in all affairs of our country. My administration shall empower Liberian women in all areas of our national life. We will support and increase the Writ of Law that restore their dignity and deal drastically with crimes that dehumanize them. We shall encourage families to educate all children, particularly the girl child.[12]

A truly determined woman will succeed in doing what society has determined she is incapable of doing.[13]

I was always battling the system to try to get to be with my people. Finally, I wouldn't work for places that kept us out. It was a damn fight everywhere I went; New York, Hollywood, all over the world.[14]

Jails and prisons are designed to break human beings, to convert the population into specimens in a zoo, obedient to our keepers, but dangerous to each other.[15]

------

[9] Isabella Bumfree (*Sojourner Truth—circa.* 1797-1883), Abolitionist and Women's Rights Advocate

[10] Coretta Scott King (1927-2006)-Wife of slain Leader, Martin Luther King, Jr. (1929-1968), Civil Rights Leader, Authoress and Activist

[11] Althea Gibson (1927-2003)-Gibson became the first Black tennis player to win Wimbledon Singles Title and the first to win the *Grand Slam* Title in 1956. She was an Authoress, Speaker and First Black to play in Ladies Professional Golf Association

[12] Ellen Johnson Sirleaf (1938-) President, Liberia, West Africa

[13] Johnnetta B. Cole, Ph.D., President Emeritus of Spelman and Bennett Colleges, Anthropologist, Authoress and Lecturer

[14] Lena Marie Calhoun Horne (1917-2010)

[15] Angela Davis (1944-)

I think children have talent and insight, but it gets beaten out of them.[16]

If society today allows wrongs to go unchallenged, the impression is created that those wrongs have the approval of the majority.[17]

A Negro woman has the same kinds of problems as other women, but see can't take the same things for granted.[18]

[16]   Rita Dove (1952-), Poet Laureate Consultant to the Library of Congress
        1993-1995; Poet Laureate of Virginia 2004-2006

[17]   Barbara Carline Jordan (1936-1996), Congresswoman

[18]   Dorothy Irene Height (1912-2010). President National Council of Negro
        Women, Administrator, Educator and Social Activist

The Hampden-Sydney Beneficial and Benevolent Society and Loving Sisters of Worship

O ye daughters of Africa, Awake! Awake! Arise!
No longer sleep nor slumber, but distinguish yourselves.[19]

Founded in 1848, thirteen years prior to the beginning of the Civil War (1861-1865), this group of Black women made an early identification of the needs of our people when such thinking was unheard of and at a time when slavery abounded in the nation. Prince Edward County had an approximate slave population of 7,341 (according to the 1860 census) and the shadows of Reverend Nat Turner's (1800-1831), rebellion in Jerusalem, Virginia on August 21, 1831, were yet cast.

But throughout the history of Africans in America, there has always been room for insurrections and resurrections of all kinds. Through a God of Deliverance and His Son of liberation, strides toward justice and equality have always been in progressive motion. American slavery and all its tentacles and power; though ungodly and inhumane, have never been so coercive to the extent wherein we could not advance the cause. A profoundly poetic statement from sister Maya Angelou (1928—) validates this theory in practice when she penned the words: "*And Still I Rise.*"

From the date of its inception, this organization of blood committed brothers and sisters have always conducted an annual gathering on the first Saturday in August. Traditionally, this has been known as the "Turn Out." Here, people come to market their productions: foods, arts, crafts etcetera.

Undergirded by a deep spiritual and religious activism, these "Saints of God" had addressed the basic survival needs, health and

---

[19] African American Folklore

burial concerns. It was from out of the generosity of organizations like this that mutual aid societies and insurance companies have sprung.

The Williams', our family, are natives of the Hampden-Sydney area. The church of attendance in this area has been The Mercy Seat Baptist Church founded in 1870. From this village, numerous Black Entrepreneurs, educators and skilled persons in the journeyman's trade industry have emerged. Socially, politically and athletically, many Blacks in this part of the county are among our most outstanding people.

The triumphs of Blacks here are due very much to the influential elements of Hampden-Sydney College founded in 1775. In sharing this thought with Ronald Heineman, Ph.D., professor emeritus in a September 2009 interview, he stated, "I am almost sure that there must have been a liberal element from the college."

Be it known that this group of motivational Christians with zeal and determination still conducts its business as usual.

The following is a description of their labors as given through their By-Laws:[20]

CONSTITUTION AND BY-LAWS OF BENEFICIAL BENEVOLENT SOCIETY AND LOVING SISERS AND BROTHERS OF

HAMPDEN-SYDNEY, VIRGINIA

ARTICLE I: NAME AND PURPOSE

SECTION I.   The name of this club shall be the Beneficial Benevolent Society and Loving Sisters of Worship of Hampden-Sydney, Virginia.

SECTION II: The purpose of this club shall be:

    A. Motto: "Keeping our History Alive"

    B. Organization will secure harmony of action and cooperation of the Society

---

[20]   As provided by Mary "Vickie" Moton-an active member

C. Raise the highest standards of home and environment

D. Encourage and promote the highest standards of learning and achievements amongst our siblings to promote excellence of learning abilities

E. Provide Bereavement Funds to help individuals and family members that have lost their loved one

F. To promote the Education of Children, Moral, Social, Religion and welfare of Families for all People

The First Baptist Church

"Where People of All Races, Political Beliefs and Religions are Welcomed"[21]

Leslie Francis Griffin, Sr. (1916-1980)

During the duration of my pastorate of First Baptist Church (1982-1986), I never lost sight and perspective of laboring under the statements by Dr. Griffin, printed on Sunday bulletins. I was Griffin's immediate successor and James P. Ashton's (current pastor) immediate predecessor. Under Ashton's leadership this statement remains as a beaconing signal to those who seek the delightful fulfillment and meaningful experiences in the context of *"lively worship."*

The name of any "First" church, regardless of its denomination, signifies that it is the earliest group of organized believers. There were many churches in the Prince Edward Community that were given spiritual and religious birth by "First Church," as has been commonly referred to by several old by-gone saints during its first 100 years. "First" is indicative of its primary status and recognition in the community.

Utilized by Griffin, this church house was an anvil to hammer out the Social Gospel of Jesus of Nazareth and render mass mobility toward making such a Gospel become realized.

A mood of self-centered distinction has always invaded the atmosphere of this church for two distinct but related reasons: First: After all, come what may, we were ***first***, and Second: We possess status, based on our professional skilled journeymen's trade, emphasizing academic and educational achievements.

---

[21]   Source: From the front of Bulletin cover by *Dr. Leslie Francis Griffin, Sr. (1916-1980); Pastor from 1949-1980.*

Sunday School and Youth Development have been the mainstay of this congregation. Reverend and Mrs. R. W. McDaniel second pastor and first lady of this house, demonstrated the earliest expression of this thought. The 1967 Centennial yearbook edition expresses it thusly: "He was a civic-minded person, always interested in seeing that the general conditions of the community were improved." Reverend Mr. McDaniel and one of his daughters, Miss H. McDaniel began operation of the McDaniel Academy. The tuition was $1.25 per session and $10.00 per month. "McDaniel Hill" located on Grove Street still bears his name.

Because of its "first-ness" and size (the largest building within a fifty-mile radius,—Court Street Baptist in Lynchburg being next), these features have always made the church a central meeting place for the community as well as for religious gatherings.

In this connection, a "**first**" study of its kind was done by William Edward Burghardt DuBois, Ph.D. (1868-1963), for the Department of Labor in January 1898. The title of this monumental effort was: *The Negroes of Farmville, Virginia: A Social Study.* "In the town of Farmville there are three colored church edifices; centered in the surrounding county there are three or four others. The chief and overshadowing organization is the First Baptist Church of Farmville. It owns a large brick edifice on Main Street. The auditorium; which seats about 500 people is tastefully furnished in light colored wood, with carpet, small organ and stained glass windows. Beneath this is a large assembly room with benches. This building is really the central clubhouse of the community, and in greater degree than is true of the country churches of New England or the West. Various organizations meet here, the church collects and distributed considerable sums of money and the whole social life of the town centers here."

During the period after the Civil War (1861-1865), when Blacks were not permitted to read, many shrewd minded Sunday school teachers grasp and utilized the idea of teaching children how to read while simultaneously teaching the Sunday school lessons. This was done of course, in clandestine fashion. Addressing this point in their superlative work entitled: *The Black Church in the African American Experience*, C. Eric Lincoln and Lawrence H. Mamiya writes: "Sunday Schools were often the first places where Black people made contact with the educational process, first hearing from memorizing, and finally, learning to read the Bible."

The First Baptist Church has therefore been a kind of learning center of sorts, fostering ideas and combining academics with spiritually. Its basement was used as a hospital during the Civil War.

Our Family

Our family lays claim on such powerful and unique generational legacy in this almost century and one half year old "Church House" that no other family can come near in resemblance or duplication!

For instance, my mother, her sister, my wife, her two sisters; my wife's sister's son and daughter; four of our five grandchildren and I were baptized in the same baptistery. And when she becomes of age, with great anticipation, I look forward to baptizing our youngest grandchild as I did the above mention four.

Furthermore, Dr. Leslie Francis Griffin performed our wedding there and I performed the weddings of our three daughters there. Dr. Griffin was the "John the Baptizer" for our children.

I preached my "Trial Sermon" at the church, December 28, 1958 four weeks after my mother died on December 2, 1958. She was a pianist; playing at the time when stricken and died three days later. Through the generous efforts of Reverend James P. Ashton and the congregation, I preached my 50th Anniversary sermon there. Finally, my mother, her sister and their parents were funeralized from this church.

Amen, Amen, and Amen!

The liberal theology preached in this church is based on the social teachings of the Nazarene, and emphasizes social action without regard of race or creed.[22]

Of Our Striven and Striving Brothers

It must be borne in mind that the tragedy of life does not lie in not reaching your goal. The tragedy of life lies in not having a goal to reach.[23]

It so happens that in our country that the very section (the south) of it, which is unquestionably the chief sea of orthodoxy, is at the same time the dependable theatre of our most heartless inhumanities.[24]

A man can't ride your back unless it's bent . . . . An individual who breaks a law that conscious tells him is unjust, and who willingly accepts the penalty of imprisonment in order to arouse the conscious

---

[22]   Source: From the back Bulletin cover by *Dr. Leslie Francis Griffin, Sr. (1916-1980)*; Pastor from 1949-1980

[23]   Benjamin Elijah Mays, Ph.D.,(1894-1984)-Clergyman, Author, Lecturer, and President of Morehouse College

[24]   Vernon Napoleon Johns (1895-1965), was Clergyman, College President and Immediate Predecessor of Dr. Martin Luther King, Jr. at the Dexter Avenue Baptist Church, and "Father of the Civil Rights Movement"

of the community over its injustice, is in realty expressing the highest respect for the law.[25].

In our so-called democracy, we are accustomed to give the majority what they want; rather than educate them to understand what is best for them.[26]

Carter Goodwin Woodson, Ph.D. (1875-1950), Educator, Author, and Founder of Negro History Week in 1926 (later becoming established as Black History Month in February, 1976) because Abraham Lincoln's birthday and that of Frederick Augustus Washington Bailey Douglass' birthdays are February 12, 1809 and February, 1818 respectively. Concerning Black History Month, A. Phillip Randolph was quoted as saying "Freedom is never given it is won." Woodson was also one of the three founders of the Association for The Study of Negro Life and History in 1915.

Up you mighty race; you can accomplish what you will.[27]

Marcus Mosiah Garvey (1887-1940), died in London and was interred there until 1964 when his remains were exhumed and brought to Jamaica, West Indies. I visited the gravesite in Jamaica, May, 2010.

When the power of love overcomes the love of power, the world will finally know peace.[28]

America will always side with those whom she can direct, give orders and have those orders obeyed.[29]

---

25 Martin Luther King, Jr., Clergyman, Author, Civil Rights Leader

26 Carter Goodwin Woodson, Ph.D. (1875-1950), Educator, Author, and Founder of Negro History Week

27 Marcus Mosiah Garvey (1887-1940), Entrepreneur, Author, Lecturer, Black Nationalist Pan Africanist

28 Johnny Allen Hendrix "Jimi" (1942-1970), musician, composer, singer, songwriter

29 Louis Eugene Walcott (Louis Farrakhan, 1933-), Supreme Minister of The Nation of Islam

Emancipate yourself from mental slavery. None but ourselves can free our minds. Get up; stand up for your rights. Get up, stand up, don't give up the fight.[30]

African Americans understand that race is not a valid biological concept; that it has no genetic validity. Stripped of the rhetoric of superiority and inferiority, the science of race is nothing but a fraud, grounded in power, privileged and violence against those who are oppressed. Yet our lives are defined and circumscribed by the brutal reality of racism, a system that denies the humanity of millions of people, limiting their education, employment, health, housing and future.[31]

White people live in two worlds: One black and the other white. Peoples of African descent live in three worlds: One black, one white and one gray. This grayness varies in shades from light to dark and amid these color variations we find our dwelling places and our various modes of survival. Herein encompasses our diabetes, hypertension, prostate disorders, major cholesterol elevation and trying most of all to strike a balance between social, economic, political, and inherent cultural contradictions! The gray area is that perilous in between, that tedious journey.

Again, in his previously quoted, *The Soul of Black Folk*, W.E. B. DuBois penned the following in this connection: "An American Negro: two souls, two thoughts, two un-reconciled strivings; two warring ideals in one dark body, whose dogged strength alone keeps it from being torn asunder." This he refers to as the "Double Consciousness."

---

[30] Robert Nesta "Bob" Marley (1945-1981), a Rastafarian, liberating Reggae musical engineer

[31] Manning Marable, Ph.D.

The Grand Fountain United Order of True Reformers

"Plan Purposely, Prepare Prayerfully; Proceed Positively; Pursue Persistently"[32]

The earliest recollections I have of the True Reformers date back to the latter 1930's and into the 1940's. My maternal grandmother, Lena Scott Johnson was a beautician in our home, specializing in many products of Madame C. J. Walker (1867-1919), the first female African American self-made millionaire in the United States.

Periodically, as different customers would come in, I recall, through childhood curiosity, "overhearing" them discuss the spiritual and political effects of this movement. Obviously I could not comprehend the structural significance of the group but I knew it was an organization that had meaning in Farmville and rural Prince Edward County and, most importantly, it helped "Colored People," as we were called then.

So far remotely removed from the actions and knowledge of this spiritual and humanitarian organization, I never entertained the slightest inkling of an idea that the day would appear when I would pen something on its behalf.

Bold and unselfish claims of this "secret" yet powerful church-extended related group were made possible. The Reverend William Washington Browne (1849-1897) was founder of this group. From out of a temperance organization, it became the most helpful army to build a spiritual and economic base theretofore witnessed. Browne was an ex-slave from Habershan County, Georgia. He stands stately among many other Black heroes and heroines in this nation as unsung contributors to our race. Browne, a clergyman, entrepreneur and organizer was of very rare distinction.

---

[32]   An African American Folklore

Browne, like Marcus Mosiah Garvey, (1887-1940), shared many of the same insights in resurrecting Black people from segregation, discrimination and oppression by teaching and training them to establish a sound economic footing for themselves. "Self-Help" was the term utilized and preached by Dr. Gregory Willis Hayes President of Lynchburg Seminary and College from 1891-1906. Dr. Madison Crenshaw Allen later propounded upon this term from 1946-1966 at the same institution.

Becoming an ordained clergyman in the Colored Methodist Church (CME), founded in 1870, Brown later aligned with the African Methodist Episcopal Church (AME—founded in 1816), because pressure from his bishop for spending large amounts of time in building The True Reformers Movement began to mount. Unlike many persons who managed to do one thing well, William Washington Browne advanced in multiple areas so as to include: Pastor, Union Army soldier, temperance organizer, student in Prairie du Wisconsin and renowned fighter against the Ku Klux Klan (which was organized in Tennessee in 1865).

This group of Good Samaritans had similarities to the aforementioned Hampden-Sydney Beneficial and Benevolent Society and Loving Sisters and Brothers of Worship; namely, they assisted Black families with sick and death benefits. It was from these and other groups that gave birth to Black Insurance Companies.

In order to demonstrate a more objective perspective, the following sources would be essential:

1. "During his travels, Browne established a sub-fountain in Richmond. In 1880 he returned to Richmond to become Grand Worthy Master of the State of Virginia, and the Richmond sub-fountain became the Grand Fountain. At the time commercial insurance companies charged African Americans higher rates than their counterparts. Assuming complete control of the True Reformers, Browne introduced such a mutual-aid benefit plan to provide life to members of the organization.

2. "Browne also created a formula by which members death benefits increased as more sub-fountains were formed and the organization grew.

3. "As the organization grew, The True Reformers opened the Savings Bank of the Grand Fountain in Richmond chartered by an Act of the General Assembly. It was the first Black-owned chartered bank in the United States. Through the bank, the True Reformers provided mortgage loans and other banking services that were difficult for African Americans to obtain. The bank opened in Browne's home on April 3, 1889.

4. "The True Reformers started a bi-monthly newspaper, *The Reformer*, which by 1900 had become a weekly publication with a circulation of more than 8,000. In 1900, the Hotel Reformer opened for business.

5. "With the death of William Washington Browne in 1897 the United Order of the True Reformers was run by a Committee. By the beginning of the twentieth century, The True Reformers had established branches in twenty-four states and had paid out more than one million in death benefits.

6. "In the midst of the Jim Crow era, the Order provided employment and business opportunities to African Americans who would otherwise have been ignored."[33]

Among the prominent sources in the history and extensive activities of True Reformism is the work of David M. Fahey titled: *The Black Lodge in White America, 'True Reformer' Browne and His Economic Strategy.*

Fahey writes as quoting from Browne: "It was and is the object of the founders of this Association, The Grand Fountain United

---

[33] Source: *Linking to Our Past: Documenting The African Americans Experience in Virginia.* The Virginia Historical Society.

Order of True Reformers, to assist our poor and heavy laden hands, hearts and heads with the care of our families in the journey of life and death.

"To assist the sick, stricken down by disease and unable to help themselves or their families; also to assist in the burial of the dead, as these are dreaded hours and great calamity to a poor family.

"There are children of a poor family left to depend upon themselves, or a poor mother with nothing to assist them or her in the hour of their sore affliction. This brings the necessity of an insurance or endowment, such as we have.

"Again, we find that the winds of adversity sometimes blow stumbling blocks across a well person's pathway as he pursues the journey of life. Such a one needs assistance also."

This shows the necessity of a bank to teach the art of saving and properly using our means for the benefit of each other when we are not using them for ourselves.

In writing concerning this outstanding organization, W.E. B. DuBois Ph.D., in the aforementioned source regarding The First Baptist Church, penned: "one of the most remarkable orders is that of the True Reformers, which has headquarters in Richmond, Virginia, conducts a bank there, and has real estate all over Virginia. There are two 'fountains' of this order in Farmville, with perhaps fifty members in all."

Clarence Herbert Bradshaw alludes to the True Reformers in the Prospect area of the County concerning the establishment of the Calvary Baptist Church in that section that: an "E. H. Anderson and Willie Allen, [were] trustees of the Silver Light Fountain No. 1325, subordinate fountain of the Grand Fountain of the United Order of True Reformers."[34]

Since high school days and especially during my Civil Rights Voter Registration work in the County, it has been my keen observation to notice that the Prospect/Pamplin areas were the leading areas in business, academics, politics and community organization.

---

[34]   Source: *History of Prince Edward County, Virginia: From its Earliest Settlements through its Establishment in 1754 to its Bicentennial Year.* The Dietz Press Incorporated, Richmond, Virginia.

They could always be depended upon almost "***first***" in most any outreaching drive that could be beneficial to our community. Lacy Ward, Jr., Executive Director of The Robert Russa Moton Museum and native to this area contends that many servicemen settled in that area following The Civil War's end in 1865, in less than ten miles from Appomattox. Ward's cousin, Catherine Scott, attributes this advancement to schools and educational interests.

In addition to their comments I have regarded the True Reformers and the Norfolk and Western Railroad as contributing components to growth of this area. More blacks were employed by the Railroad in the Prospect/Pamplin area than any other area in the county. This area is populated by the Allen, Berryman, Hendricks and Scott families amid others of great prominence. The prosperity of any settlers in this area is highly encouraged due to the fact that the soil type of the Prospect/Pamplin area is highly conducive to agricultural success.[35]

---

[35] Source: Andrea L. Bridge, copy editor, geologist, environmentalist, historian, vocalist, friend and author "*Closing the Loop: Recycling, Reformation and Reuse in Prince Edward, Amelia, Buckingham and Cumberland Counties*", 2002

The Martha E. Forrester Council of Colored Women

Founded: 1920

Motto: "Lifting as we climb."

A native Richmonder and public school teacher in that city, Martha E. Forrester (1863-1951), possessed brilliance beyond boundaries!

My recollection of her is that of a tall towering figure, quite stately and elegant in her stride as she rocked from side to side. Her physique symbolized strength and readiness. Whenever one was graced by her presence, one knew that he or she was in the company of a seriously sincere sister, sanctified in truth and the educational development of our people.

So familiar was Martha E. Forrester with the intentional and oppressive lack of educational opportunities among "Colored People," as promoted by a white racist paternalistic system, she organized a Cadre of five women in order to construct a movement that would eventually build a new high school for Colored Children. Such a task was completed in 1939. It was erected to accommodate one hundred eighty students but four hundred fifty came for attendance at its initial opening. Named in honor and distinction of an adjoining Amelia County native, Robert Russa Moton (1867-1940), this high school is one of the five foundational stones used in the 1954 Brown vs. Board of Education Supreme Court Decision. The remaining "Test Cases" were: Wilmington, Delaware; Clarendon, South Carolina; Topeka, Kansas; and Washington, D.C.

As written in their *"History of The Martha E. Forrester Council of Women,"* the word "Colored" was eliminated and males included in 1996, it is obviously evident that these daughters of faith, fire and fortitude were deeply committed in addition to the erection of a new academic facility.[36] Their purposes are disclosed as follows; on April 6, 1920, a band of five dedicated women agreed to unite for the following reasons:[37]

1. "To furnish systematic help for the uplift of the Negroes in our community.
2. To improve educational advantages for the Negroes of this community.
3. To secure harmony of action and cooperation among the people of Farmville.
4. To improve the home life, the morals and civic life of our people.
5. To administer to the less fortunate."

The founders agreed to solicit other interested citizens. Seventeen women answered the call for united action in order to improve and reach all segments of community life.

The following sisters were among the originals: Mesdames Ida Allen, Nannie Harvey, Addie Holmes, Annie Miller, Margaret Ward and Katie Wiley.[38] I possess a vivid recollection of each of the stalwart leaders. During the mid-late 20's, my grandmother, Lena Scott Johnson and during the mid-1940, my mother Nannie Johnson Butler became members.

As written on a photograph, now located in the Robert Russa Moton Museum; "This group of women spent thousands of hours in community service. They have worked with tutoring, bloodmobiles, counseling and other projects as they live out their motto: "*Lifting as we climb*."[39]

Finally, the Forrester Council was one of the affiliate Chapters of the National Council of Negro Women organized by Mary McLeod Bethume (1875-1955) in 1935. Dorothy Irene Height (1912-2010), was President for forty years.

---

36   Source: *Edwilda Allen*, an active member and former student
37   Source: *The Moton Museum*
38   Source: *Edwilda Allen*, an active member and former student
39   Source: *The Moton Museum*

PART II

The Magnetization of Black Churches Relative to Interfaith Action and Response

The Intervening of Divine Mysticism

History is a subject only relevant to a people interested in:
1. Seeking identity, 2. Maintaining culture, 3. Fighting for the collective survival.[40]

People who dislike history do so primarily on the basis of dates that are to be recalled and the irrelevancy of those dates and events to the present. This, however, is but one angle of history as we know it to be. Many view this as a "waste of time", as I heard my wife, Ann, discuss with our son-in-law Isaac, on one occasion in a general conversation.

The above view does contain an element of truth but this should not be considered the terminus point. Rather, history should be visualized as objectively as possible, encompassing a broad sweep of occurrences connecting interrelated events and persons. Thus, the past becomes the future's light being held at any given moment in the present.

History is an unfolding drama of the acts and doings of people in a broad-based sweeping range of events. That which has happened (the past), is inseparable from the dimensions of the present and that which is destined by God to appear in its unfolding. However, with God these dimensions are non-existent. "For a thousand years in your sight are like yesterday, when it is past, or like a watch in the night."[41] Or "But do not ignore this one fact, beloved, that with the Lord one day is like a thousand years, and a thousand years are like one day."[42]

The intervening of the providence in establishing the Modern Civil Rights Movement was buttress upon Plessey versus Ferguson (1896). From this case, Brown versus The Board of Education was birthed. "Brown", as it is referred to, was litigated to form five

---

[40]   Alton H. Maddox, Jr.-*Amsterdam News,* April 14, 2005
[41]   Psalm 90: 4 New Revised Standard Version
[42]   2 Peter 3:8 New Revised Standard Version

"Test Cases": Clarendon, South Carolina; Topeka, Kansas; Prince Edward County, Virginia; Wilmington, Delaware; and Washington, The District of Columbia, in that specific order.

One of the numerous ways history becomes alive to us is not merely through the memorization of dates per se, but making comparisons and contrasts with those dates and occurrences in order to obtain knowledge and extend our perspectives of the future march of history. History cannot be separated from occurrences; they are the **Mother of History** itself.

The vicissitudes of history tell of its paths that are cyclic and linear. Along these paths, the vicissitudes of our lives keep us moving in the flow of our being, both in favor of, yet against our sojourn.

Every action precipitates a reaction as in the Hegelian Dialectic of thesis, antithesis and synthesis.

History also informs us that no person is born ahead of his or her time. In my possession is a bumper sticker from The Quest Book Store in Charlottesville, Virginia which states: *"Everything in the Universe is subject to change and everything is on schedule."* Change and scheduling are ordered Divinely.

Thus, an assignment is hereby given to fulfill the thoughts of the first paragraph (above), discerning and reconciling the ebb and flow of Black History made in America.

The Central Committee

Following the conclusion of World War II (1939-1945), there went out throughout the land, a clarion call to racially integrate public facilities. President Harry S. Truman issued an executive mandate on this account, Executive order #9981, on July 26, 1948. Briefly, it stated that all armed forces were to integrate all personnel. He has been given credit for such action. But, be reminded that he did not act on his own volition or his having volunteered. Asa Phillip Randolph (1889-1979), founder and president of The Brotherhood of Sleeping Car Porters, his accomplice, Grant Reynolds and others; coerced the president into such action through the "threat" of protest and demonstrations in the nation's capital.

The atmosphere toward the integrationists' mood spread to the County of Prince Edward. But this was not our primary concern. "Separate and equal" was the end product of the students as we protested.

A Central Committee was established by Barbara Johns and immediate activists classmates. This hub, in addition to Reverend L. Francis Griffin, Civil Rights lawyers and others were the source around which the movement revolved.

The Committee was composed of students who possessed leadership potential and courage, thus naming the entire ordeal, **The Manhattan Project**. It was the nucleus of the movement.

Of Barbara Rose Johns' performing
A Wedding between Courage and Conviction

I love to see a young girl go out and grab the world by the lapels. Life's a bitch. You've got to go out and kick ass."—Maya Angelou (1928—)

Protesting Pupils

Barbara Johns, Vernon's niece, was my classmate, that serene fire and "prophetess Deborah" of our movement to initiate a burning force not to integrate racially per se, but to lead us in striking for state-of-the-art facilities of that day. With all of the zeal and dogged determination, she led forth with the torch a flame that the aforementioned Martha E. Forrester and others had given her in the Spirits of God, Church and Moton. As Emmett Louis Till (1941-1955), was the child catalyst and catharsis of the modern Civil Rights Movement, so was Barbara in a different setting!

She certainly encompasses the Johns' mystique as stated by her Aunt Altona Trent Johns, Vernon's wife, and our elementary school teacher of profound musical talent, when she wrote concerning her husband: "He came from two families who possessed frank and independent ideas and were not afraid to express them to members of both races upon provocation."[43]

Thus, much of Barbara Johns' actions were genetic, an integral part of her deoxyribonucleic acid (DNA) called for the perpetuation of such actions which culminated in a student strike on April 23, 1951. In his publication, *Students on Strike: Jim Crow, Civil Rights, Brown and Me: A Memoir,* John A. Stokes penned: "The strike was the brainchild of Barbara Johns. She had read about how some white students at a girl's school up north had gone on strike to get better dining room facilities. It had worked for them, so she was determined to make it work for us."

Barbara's initial move was to contact Miss Inez Davenport, the music teacher, concerning the inequities and deplorable conditions of our total educational facilities. Davenport planted the seed of revolution by raising one persuasive question: *"Well, why don't you do something about it?"* This was done clandestinely. The nature of this question was also raised biblically by Queen Esther's cousin (not Uncle as many proclaim), Mordecai. When her family was on the verge of annihilation, and most Jews were threatened, Mordecai proposed a persuasive question: *"Think not that in the King's palace you will escape any more than all the other Jews. For if you keep silence at such a time as this, relief and deliverance will rise for the Jews from another quarter, but you and your father's house will perish. And who knows whether or not you have come into the Kingdom at such a time as this?"* Queen Esther's response:*Then I will go to the King, though it is against the law; and if I perish, I perish".*[44]

Of all the names that could have been given to her "home church," in Darlington Heights, Virginia, the name "***Triumph***" was selected. It is from out of this church house that the Johns family attended; a name descriptive of prevailing and succeeding as the reader can imagine. Such is a legacy that all persons that I know and have known from ***Triumph*** march to the beat of its cadence. One of the leading churches in the county in civil rights and social

---

43 Source: *Human Possibilities: A Vernon John s Reader.* Samuel Lucius Gandy, Editor of, Hoffman Press, 1977

44 Esther 4:13-B-14; 16-C Revised Standard Version

equality, it was founded in 1878. All of its clergymen are pictured on the walls of its fellowship hall.

Following much litigation from attorneys: Thurgood Marshall (1908-1993); Oliver White Hill (1907-2001); Spottswood William Robinson (1916-1998); and Martin A. Martin, students attended the New Robert Russa High School in September 1953. Prince Edward County became one of the five "Test Cases," used to comprise The Supreme Court's 1959 Brown vs. Board of Education. The remaining four: Topeka, Kansas; Clarendon, South Carolina; Wilmington, Delaware; and Washington, D.C.

"Attorneys with the NAACP filed suit on their behalf, not merely to gain improved school facilities but as a broader challenge to the prevailing "separate but equal" doctrine, and thus to the laws and customs that supported segregated public education throughout the south."[45]

1. "It's almost like reaching for the moon."[46]
2. "Without some fixed point outside myself, I cannot exist."[47]
3. "It is one thing to be admired, and another to be the guiding star which saves the anguish."[48]

---

[45] Source: *The Newsletter for The Virginia Foundation for the Humanities*—Fall 2010.
[46] Barbara Johns, 1935-1991
[47] Henrik Ibsen, 1828-1906
[48] Soren Kierkegaard, 1813-1855

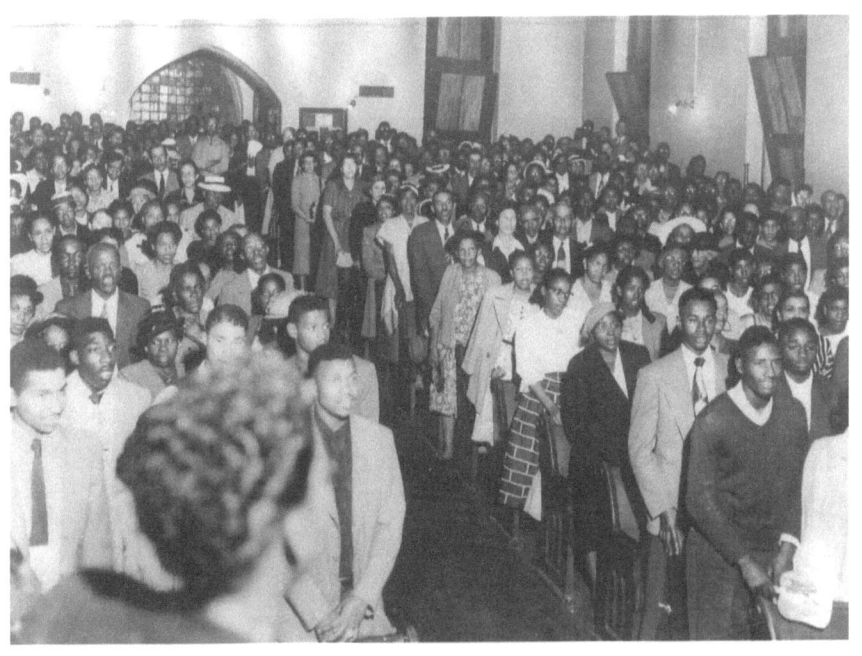

The last NAACP rally at historic First Baptist Church in
Farmville, Virginia. 1951.
(J. Samuel Williams is pictured third row on the right, light
jacket.)
Photo provided by the Afro-American Newspapers of
Baltimore, Md.

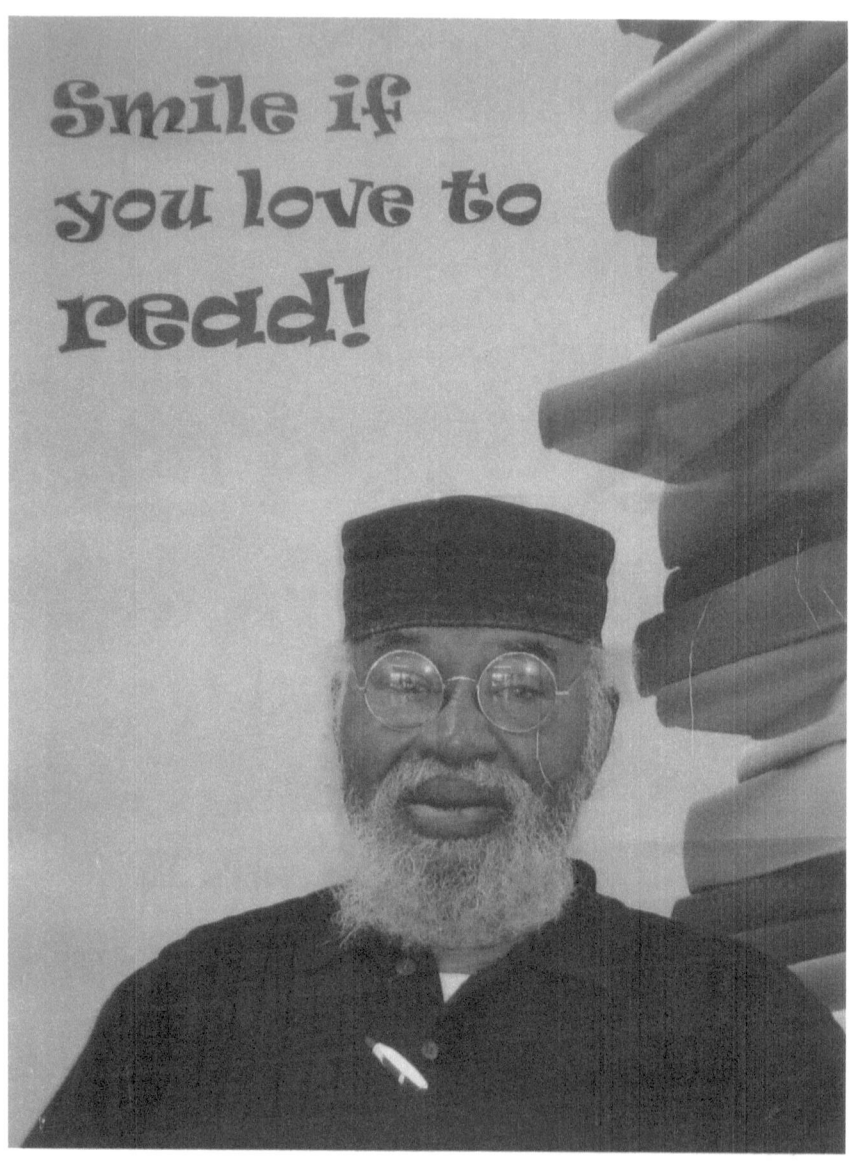

Taken on April 13, 2011-Farmville Prince Edward Library.
National Library Week.
Photo of me taken by Peggy Epperson, Executive Director of
Library

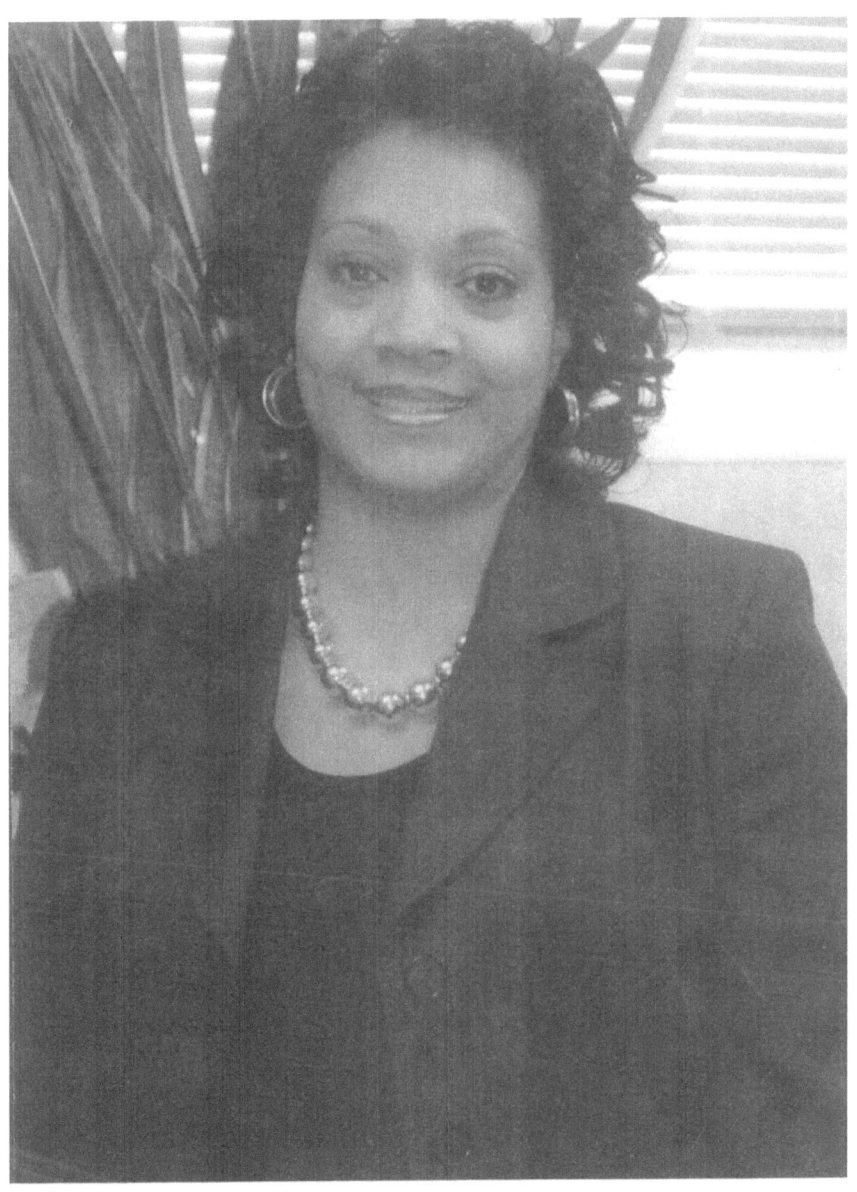

Machelle J. Eppes, Prince Edward County's First Black Circuit Court Clerk; serving since 2005.

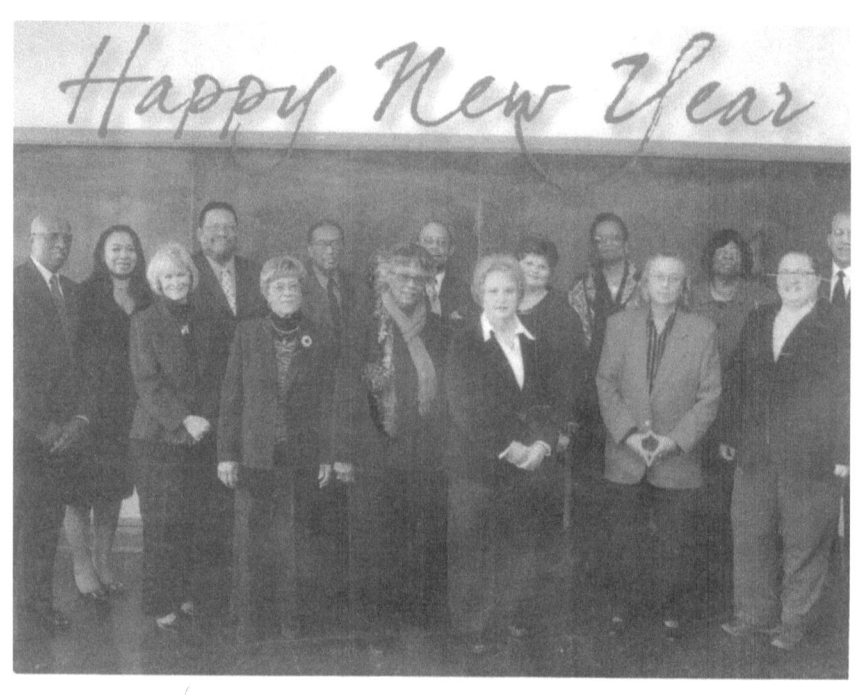

Board of Directors-Robert R. Moton Musuem. 2009.

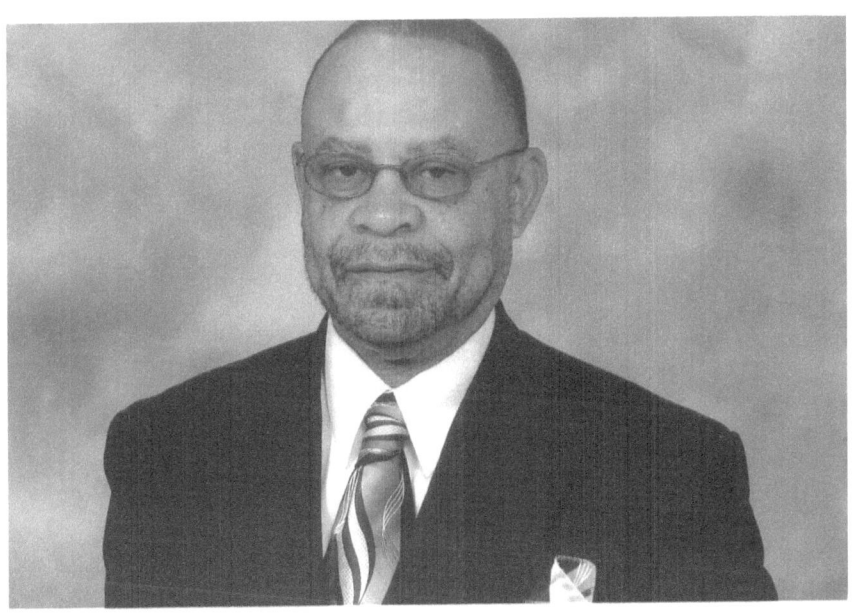

Armstead Douglas "Chuckie" Reid-First Black Vice Mayor of
Farmville, Virginia. serving since the early 1980s

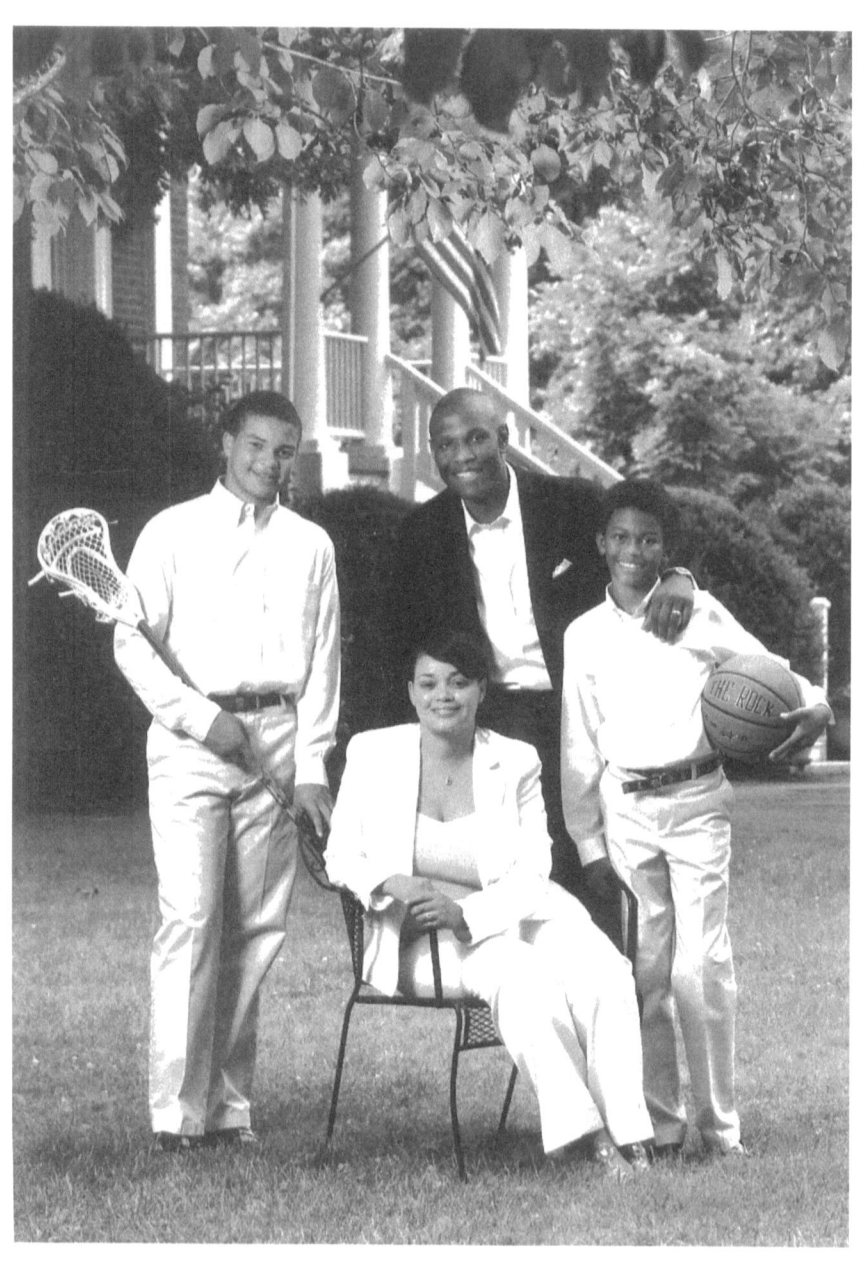

Dr. and Mrs. Christopher B. Howard and family. First Black
president of Hampden-Sydney College.

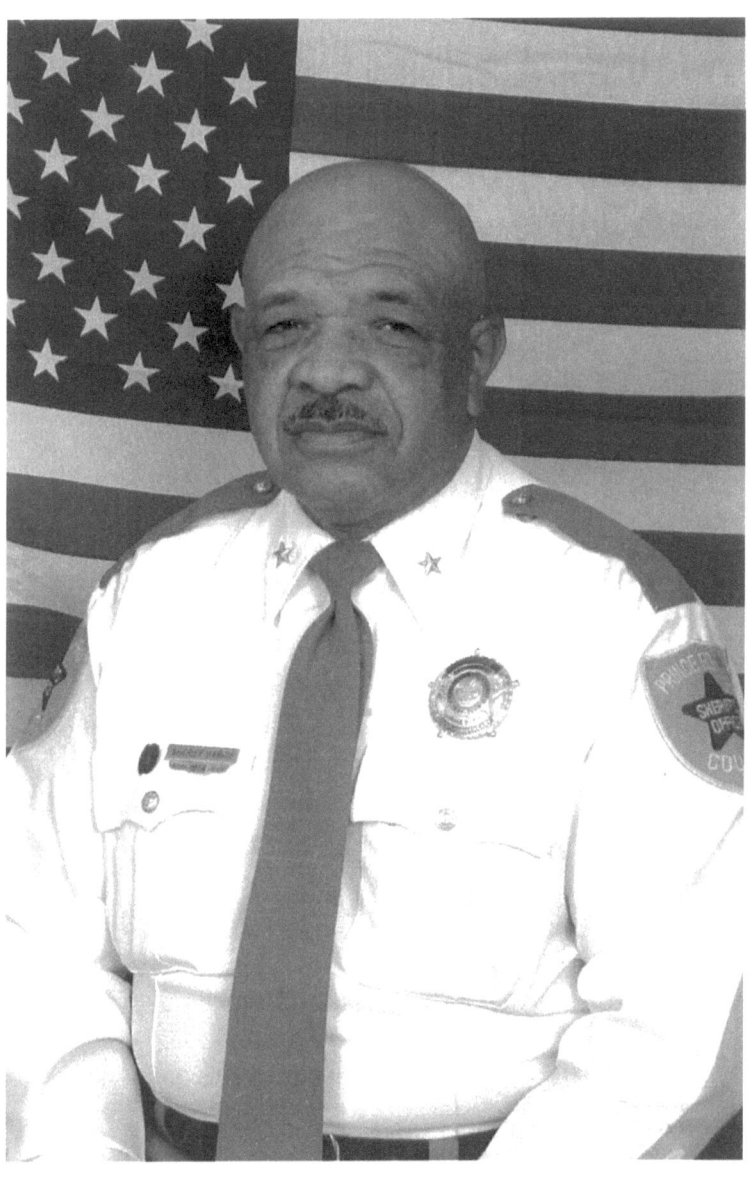

Travis D. Harris-First Black County Sheriff. Harris will complete his second term in December 2011.

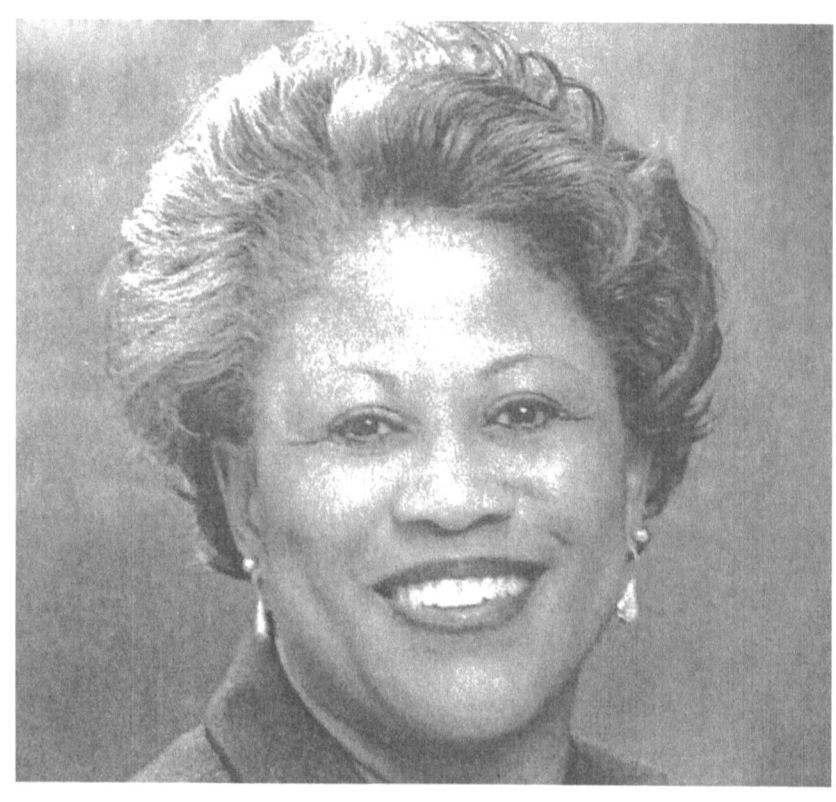

Bernice Smith-First Black Branch Manager (Bank of America) in
Prince Edward County
Smith began her banking career in the early 1980s

Leslie Francis Griffin, Sr.
1916-1980

Everything about life is a legitimate concern of my religion.

Occasionally, people raise the questions: **Why such a time as this in world history? Why not earlier or later?** My playmate of the 1930's elementary and high school classmate and one of the original leaders of the movement, John Watson, attributes this to "Divine Intervention."

And this is precisely that which Griffin assisted us in initiating. In coordination of this Divine encounter, a "new prophet of radical and social righteousness underground" as I often referred to him was, as "John The Baptizer, Sent from God."

Succeeding his father, Charles Henry Dinston Griffin in 1949, as pastor of the historic First Baptist Church in Farmville, he preached, prophesied, and taught a Social Gospel, which was, applying the Social and Ethical teachings of Jesus of Nazareth to social problems in society. Thus, he gave us, as it were, a "New Jesus!"

He, un-liked and unaccepted by many, including some of his congregants, challenged Black churches to enter into a realm of racial consciousness as pertaining to our efforts as protesting pupils to the degree of total involvement. Outside the confines of the church's walls, his being deeply entrenched in The National Association for the Advancement of Colored People (founded in 1901 in New York City) and President of the Parent Teacher's Association (PTA), gave him unique but broad perspective which transcended the expectations of the average minister. Griffin did not adjust or adapt, to the required mold of preachers *period.* Even during his teenage years, the late Reverend James Brown of Hampden-Sydney and pastor of Mercy Seat Baptist Church in Hampton, Virginia said of him: "When Leslie was growing up among us, he was different." He was also special consultant to the NAACP and later becoming its state president.

Griffin stood stalwart as our leader nurturing the seed to grow that had been planted in Barbara Johns' mind by our music teacher Miss Inez Davenport, clandestinely. Davenport later became the wife of our principal, M. Boyd Jones, a principal with a principle! A team of Griffin, Jones and John Lancaster (local Farm Demonstration Agent) and member of The First Baptist Church-attended regularly by Jones, formed a triumphant trio in our struggle for justice and equality. For their unswerving commitment, the latter two were eventually fired, but obtained meaningful employment in other portions of the state and nation.

The inquiry is always brought to light by questioning strengths, weaknesses and future of a movement of this character. For instance, Why? Why now? Is it feasible? All of the questions and answers will never be known in a social movement because "We walk by faith and not by sight." (2 Corinthians 5:7). In other words, this intervening of the Divine is shared by David M. Fahey, in writing concerning The True Reformers: "One of the strangest things about the ways of Divine Providence is the leading of His children into paths that outwardly appear to be avenues of ill and misfortune, and yet are always found working out His own Divine purpose for the good of His chosen."[49]

As my "Father in the Ministry" for 22 years and 22 months and my pastor for 30 years; of his brilliance, social ethics, and courageousness, I do declare:

> . . . *My Father, My Father the [mighty] chariot of Israel, and the horsemen thereof!*[50]

---

[49]   Source: *The Black Lodge in White America: "True Reformer" Browne and His Economic Strategy*

[50]   2 Kings 12 RSV

Interfaith and Interracial Collaborations

Open Minds vs. Closed Schools
1959-1964

Truth is one, paths are many.—Sri Swami Satchidananda
(1914-2002)

In their June 2, 1959 monthly meeting, the Prince Edward County Board of Supervisors voted unanimously to discontinue public education in the county rather than comply with a federal mandate to integrate all facilities.

What price did such a white racist paternalistic board have to pay for such defiance? Absolutely nothing! Local status quo "owners" of the county in surreptitious action with elected officials, the Fourth Circuit Court, the backlash blast of Senator Harry Flood Byrd's "Massive Resistance" oppressive forces and The Southern Manifesto worked influentially and interchangeably under the deceptive false phrase, "With all deliberate speed," as written by the U.S. Supreme Court.

This historic decision did not pass as a powerful landslide victory. In principle and practice, southern Senators and the House of Representatives struck grave opposition to the decision. In this connection, Jonathan Birnbaum and Clarence Taylor wrote: "Southern Senators and Representatives condemned Brown with the 'Southern Manifesto.' Throughout the south there was massive, State endorsed resistance, including a grand assault on The NAACP, crushing the group's activity and membership. A single court ruling would not decide the struggle. As Melissa Fay Green writes, "'Civil Rights was not a one-time event . . . . It had to be fought for in every little community'!"

Moreover, they wrote: "The Southern Manifesto, a segregationist response to the Supreme Court's decision in Brown vs. Board, was signed by nineteen southern Senators and eighty-two Members of the House of Representatives.[51]

Whenever a group or groups organizes around an idea (s) that stresses resources and mobilization of that idea for the furtherance and betterment of Oppressed People, many other groups of great interest and concern are magnetized toward such endeavors.

This was the situation of human equality and social justice when public education was denied rather than integrate facilities as demanded by federal law. The county of Prince Edward became victims of such circumstance.

Political, religious groups and organizations have similarities, differences and all *points in between. Science, Theologies, Philosophies, and other disciplines extract various* strands and beliefs from each other. No complete body of knowledge stands stately in solidarity stature and thus all of life is bound inextricably. God created the universe in such an interwoven state of eternal and internal existence!

During the turbulent school closing years, there emerged upon the scene denominational religious bodies and church related constituents that contributed immensely to the moment through their presence and financial assistance.

Some among those are: The Baptists Allied Bodies (now The Baptist General Convention of Virginia), Reverends Charles L. Evans and Caesar L. Scott, Executive Directors, respectively; The Student Non-Violent Coordination Committee (SNCC); and the Hasadiah Baptist Association founded in 1874.

From a broader perspective, Reverend L. Francis Griffin, Sr. states: "There are many individuals and organizations to which we owe a debt of gratitude. However, the following have been the greatest source of financial aid to date: The National Council of Negro Women, The American Friends Service Committee, The Delta Sigma Theta Sorority, Inc., The Ministerial Alliance of Newark, New Jersey and vicinity, the Ministerial Alliance of Washington, D.C., The Ministerial Alliance of Northern Virginia at Falls Church, Virginia, The Grand Temple Daughters of Elks, I.B.O.E. of W., The

---

[51]   Source: *Civil Rights: A Reader on the Black Struggle Since 1787*

Virginia Funeral Directors Association and several branches of the NAACP Virginia State Conference of Branches."[52]

    With these thoughts in our conscience, let us focus upon the "multiple multitudes," who journeyed their way to Prince Edward and became contributors of the Divinely mystical purposes for which they were called and chosen. In order that the reader may comprehend their efforts, I have included some tenants of each church or organization to demonstrate the interrelatedness thereof.

---

52   Source: *Prince Edward County Christian Association; Operation 1700, Special Report*, May 9, 1960

American Friends Service Committee
(Quakers also Friends)
Founder: George Fox
1624-1691

Since it's founding, The American Friends Service Committee, also loosely referred to as "Quakers," have been in the forefront battling in favor of abolitionism, peace, social justice, love and racial equality. They made their way into Prince Edward County as early as the mid-Nineteenth Century.

During the harsh and bitter school closing years, Jean Fairfax was one leading Black Quaker who organized with great diligence and commitment, monumental efforts in bringing God to parents and children by opening the doors of academia. It was as if she responded to three biblical mandates: ***Note: The three biblical passages below are NRSV translations.**

1. My people are destroyed for lack of knowledge.—Hosea 4:6*
2. Truly I tell you, just as you did it to one of the least of those who are members of my family, you did it to me.—Matthew 25:4*
3. Come over to Macedonia and help us.—Acts 16:9*

In his masterpiece work published, Bob Smith regarding the entire sweep of the movement and specifically the work of the subject now under our own thinking; he wrote: "When the American Friends Service Committee (AFSC) went to work in Prince Edward County, Virginia in 1959, it responded to the Black parents who said, 'We want our children to have some education they can't just sit here while white children go to the academies.' The American Friends Service Committee (AFSC) conducted an emergency placement program that placed young Black students from Prince Edward with families in six states and ten communities. This was the AFSC's human response.

"....Our work in Prince Edward County was an important chapter in AFSC's eighty-year commitment to establish freedom from social and economic injustice for all members of our global society. We continue to work in partnership with communities throughout the world as they struggle to dismantle systems of exploitation and oppression and to establish an open and non-exploitative society, which recognizes the infinite worth of each human being. That is the principle on which the AFSC, established by members of the Religion Society of Friends (Quakers) is founded."[53]

The nineteenth century marked a time when many Quakers moved from the New England states and Pennsylvania to the mid-western and southern parts of the nation. They engaged themselves in abolitionists' activities of various kinds, organized elementary, high schools and colleges. As an example, the Christiansburg Institute in Christiansburg, Virginia was founded in 1866, a school for Black students, the first of this kind in Southwestern Virginia. The facility had to close in compliance with federal laws to integrate. Charles S. Schaeffer of The Freeman's Bureau founded it.

During the eulogy of Atlanta's first Black mayor, Maynard Holbrook Jackson, Jr. (1938-2002), former President William Jefferson Clinton (1946—), stated that he was asked: "Why do Black people like you?" His response was: "This is not about rocket science, Black people like those who like them." In our struggle against segregation, discrimination and all forms of oppression, we "take sides" with those who "take sides" with us in favor of "the cause and the movement."

Therefore, the following Blacks, and there are countless others, sung and unsung, who were Quakers:

Cyrus Bustill (1732-1804)
Born a slave, later became abolitionist leader and entrepreneur
Black, White and of Native American descent

---

53   Source: *They Closed Their Schools*

Paul Cuffee (1759-1817)
Businessman, Ship builder, Captain, Abolitionist and Philanthropist

Vera Green Ph.D. (1928-1982)
Anthropologist, Authoress, and Educator

Bayard Rustin (1912-1987)
Non-violent activist, Civil Rights Activist, Organizer 1957 Prayer Pilgrimage for Freedom March and the 1963 Freedom March—both in Washington, D.C.

St. Clair Drake (1911-1990)
Anthropologist, Social Scientist, Author, and a Native of Suffolk, Virginia

The writer desires the reader to research the above so that knowledge will be increased and research for other Black members of The American Friends Service Committee (AFSC), will be obtained.

By studying these religious bodies and making the recommended similarities and differences, it should not be surprising to know that Susan Brownell Anthony (1820-1906), a white woman and strong advocate for Women's Rights and Abolitionists was both Quaker and Unitarian.

Religiously, most of the New England abolitionists can be categorized as Quakers or Unitarians or Transcendentalists. Some were Deists.

Quaker Beliefs

Religious beliefs, worship patterns and practices vary according to Divine Revelations, cultures, climatic condition and other components.

Quakers often worship in silence. In this state, one may "speak out" as the Spirit specifies. Quietude is their general mode of existence.

With these brief concepts in mind, give serious consideration to most of their practices buttressed upon the following beliefs!

1. They do not have a universal governing creed.
2. They are governed by their own ethics and personal faith.
3. They range from evangelical to liberal Christians.
4. Possess a strong and firm conviction regarding pacifism
5. The element of God's existence abides in every human soul.
6. Belief in the "Inner Light" that abides in everyone
7. All persons have inherent worth independent of their gender, race, age, nationality, religion and sexual orientation.
8. Each person has a direct experience with God.
9. Christian love and goodness and a concern for the suffering and unfortunate
10. Continued Revelations through the Holy Spirit
11. A sacramental aspect of life dwells in all.
12. No difference between the sacred and the secular
13. Women are of equal status to men.
14. Speak truth at all times
15. Do not believe to Oath taking

The Nation of Islam (NOI)
Founders
Noble Drew Ali (1886-1929)
Wallace Dodd Fard (1877-?)

With no more than a dearth of sound a valid knowledge of the Nation of Islam, it should not take anyone by surprise in knowing that the Nation would summon some of its adherents to elevate the spirit and conscience levels of Blacks when public schools were non-operative.

They conducted weekly sessions in the near-eastern location of the county known as Rice. These "brothers" would come in to instruct principles, activities and the "Pillars of Islam." During a September 21, 2009 interview with Robert Hamlin, an out of school student at that time, (1959-1964), he informed me that four Muslims (one who submits to God), "Brothers" Charles and Eddie X remained about four years or more, but brother Redell X and Louis X returned to Philadelphia, Pennsylvania. They taught Black History and how to feel proud of ourselves. Also they taught "The Pillars of Islam." They were very committed and persistent in their deliberations. Once a week police would come to his residence in Rice, and say "Just checking to see if everything is alright." Such "just checkings" became such an annoyance; another location was sought and obtained.

Since then Mr. Hamlin has been chairman of The Board of Directors of The Robert Russa Moton Center for Study in Civil Rights Education. It was begun as such in 1996.

Just in passing, it is worthy of note that one of the outstanding criticisms of the Nation of Islam is that of straying away from Islamic (Orthodox) teachings and embracing Black racial awareness. They contend that race; as propounded by them is not part and parcel of Islamic thought. The Nation began this racial policy because of how Blacks were treated in Detroit and Chicago by white racists.

My usual response to such unbalanced inquiry is that, neither was slavery, racial prejudice, oppression, segregation and discrimination a part of Christianity, but under a false pretext, the slave master and mistress blended this in as a matter of controlling slaves.

And, as of this writing, the release of this control is yet to appear. Remember that Martin Luther King, Jr. (1929-1968), often reminded us that the most segregated hour in America is 11:00 o'clock on Sunday mornings!

There is a close kinship and connection between tenants of The Nation of Islam (NOI) and beliefs of the Bahá'ís, Quakers and Unitarian Universalists, a sense of non-restraint, freedom and liberation exists among them. Thus, consider some policies to which the Nation adhere.

What Muslims Want

1. We want freedom. We want a free, complete freedom.
2. We want justice, equal justice under the law. We want justice applied equally regardless of creed, class or color.
3. We want equality of opportunity.
4. We want our people in America whose parents or grandparents were descendants from slaves to be allowed to establish a separate state or territory of their own.
5. We want freedom of all believers of Islam not held in federal prison.
6. We want an immediate end to police brutality and mob attacks against the so-called Negroes throughout the United States. These are six of eight of their "wants." The following are six of their thirteen beliefs.

What Muslims Believe

1. We believe in one God whose proper name is Allah.
2. We believe in the Holy Koran and in the scriptures of all the prophets of God.

3. We believe in the truth of the Bible, but we believe it has been tampered with and must be reinterpreted so that mankind will not be snared by the falsehoods that have been added to it.
4. We believe in Allah's prophets and the scriptures they brought to the people.
5. We believe that we who declared ourselves to be righteous Muslims should not participate in wars, which take the lives of humans.
6. We believe our women should be respected as the women of other nationalities are respected and protected.[54]

All the Civil Rights organizations and liberal religions marched to the same cadence: that of freedom. But the Nation of Islam was to these United States; the same as the word of God is to humanity, "Indeed the Word of God is alive and active, sharper than any two-edged sword, piercing until it divides soul from spirit, joints from marrow, it is able to judge the thoughts and intentions of the heart."[55] And as I recall, the Nation of Islam (NOI), was the "Burning Spear" of the Civil Rights Movement.

A native of New Zealand, Noble Drew Ali was founder of The Moorish Science Temple of America in Newark, New Jersey. This religion was established in 1913.

During the educational uprisings in Prince Edward County, an adherent to Moorish Religion met with the Farmville Minister's Alliance weekly.

His name was Bey. Brother Bey was very advanced in applying Moorish beliefs to the Civil Rights struggles. He taught that Moorish Religion had its roots in Spain. The Moors were of African descent, a very ingenious, highly cultured and productive people.

The Nation of Islam (NOI), originated in Moorish Islamic Religion, having been founded in 1930 in Detroit, Michigan by W. D. Fard, who later passed the leadership to Elijah Muhammad.

---

[54] Source: *From Black Muslims to Muslims: The Resurrection Transformation and Change of the Lost-Found Nation of Islam in America*, (1930-1995), Clifton E. Marsh

[55] Hebrew 4:12 NRSV.

The Unitarian Universalist Church
(Principles)
Founder: Michal Sevetus (1511-1553)

A. The inherent worth and dignity of every person; every person is important.
B. Justice, equality and compassion for all relations
C. Acceptance of one another and encouragement to spiritual growth in our congregations
D. A free responsible search for truth and meaning
E. The right conscious and the use of democratic process within our congregations and in society at large
F. The goal of world community with peace, liberty and justice for all; and
G. Respect for the independent web of all existence of which we are a part.[56]

My attraction to Unitarians Universalists is due to their humanistic stance in relating to and feeling an integral part of people as persons.

While employed as Director of the Department of Social Service for the Buffalo (New York) Council of Church and Erie County, I became deeply entrenched as an ecumenist, the basis of which began in Prince Edward County and expanded to my matriculations at Shaw University and The School of Religion (now The Samuel DeWitt Proctors School of Theology at Virginia Union University). Although both are Baptist schools basically, their extensive liberal arts curriculum promoted interdisciplinary thinking.

This type of curriculum caused my theological thinking to become elasticized. I was not considered a stranger while in

---

[56] Source: *Meet the Unitarians* by Jack Menelson.

attendance of Buffalo's Unitarian Universalist Church, or any denominational House of God.

Following a near deathly racial incident, I organized Buffalo's first Interfaith Inter-racial Council to address and combat problems on a race based level.

Given to me at this time was an "Ecumenical Award," the only such award given to a Protestant by Catholics in this country, at that time (1973). This produced a peculiar oneness that had not been felt theretofore, among the "the brethren!"

Unitarian Universalists were begun as Unitarians in 1825. In 1961, it became the Unitarian Universalist Association. This was a consolidation of the American Universalist Association and the Universalist Church of America.

Black and white Unitarian Universalist who labored in Prince Edward's vineyard brought with them an unorthodox practical Christianity. Although non-believers in "The Trinity" as commonly expressed by most Christians, they take this position because of its "absence" from the Bible. To them, the human aspect of Jesus of Nazareth is stressed versus the Divine.

Black Unitarians

Frances Ellen Watkins Harper (1825-1911)—abolitionist, writer, a founder of the National Association of Colored Women, had a long affiliation with AME Church but was a member of First Unitarian Church of Philadelphia.

William G. Sinkford (1946—),—was the First Black President of Unitarian Universalist Church. He was a Cum Laude Graduate from Harvard and graduate of Starr King School for Ministry.

The Baha'i Faith

Founded in 1853 in Persia (today Iran), by Bah 'a U'llah (1817-1892), whose title means "The Glory of God." "Bahi" is Arabic for "Followers of the Glory." Bah' a U'llah was exiled and imprisoned most of his life because of the faith he professed. In the sight of God, he taught that all people are equal, that all religions are one and that the world is entering an era in which oneness of humanity will eventually be recognized and fully established.[57]

The beliefs of the Baha'i are as follows:

Unity of God
Unity of Religion
Unity of Humankind
Equality between Men and Women
Elimination of all form of prejudice
World Peace
Harmony of Religion and Science
Independent Investigation of Truth
Universal Compulsory Education
Universal Auxiliary Language
Non-Involvement in Partisan Politics
Elimination of Extremes of Wealth and Poverty

Many Baha'is rendered their services in assisting through teaching during the period of school.

Glenford Eckelton Mitchell, Ph.D. (1936—) was a fellow classmate at Shaw University. A native of Jamaica, West Indies, he sat on the governing body of the Universal House of Justice in Haifa, Israel. He is the only Black Bahai of national acclaim of whom I have known.

---

[57] See: *Encyclopedia of Religious Freedom*-Catherine Cookson, Editor, page: 7

The Prince Edward County Christian Association

Founded: 1960

The National Association for the Advancement of Colored People (founded in New York City in 1909) was a familiar mainstay to Blacks in the county. They had been well established since the student-led strike on April 23, 1951. But, a more indigenous organization was needed because of family and church kinship on our own soil.

People needed to establish and participate in a grass root movement and develop that kind of conscious platform and paradigm.

Such an organization gave all Black churches the chance to become participants in multiple ways. As an example, some churches became teaching centers for children who were not schooled, area community meetings and voter registration drives. The Reverend Calvin Hill, a resident of the county and pastor of churches in adjoining counties, lent his leadership through the Farmville Minister's Association (All Black), and the Hasadiah Baptist Association founded 1874. The latter covers a radius of fifty plus miles. With limited resources in much needed areas, Reverend Griffin and other Black county clergy, met the needs in areas previously mentioned and exceeded their own expectations in educational outreach. The followings statements will give the reader much intellectual food for thinking skills and tactics in community organization.

"The Prince Edward Christian Association was formed to meet an unprecedented crisis. However, its organizers envisioned the Association as not only meeting the current crisis in a satisfactory manner, but also extending it as a permanent organization into the whole life of the community after the County has returned to spiritual, political and educational sanity. The Prince Edward County Christian Association does not exist to replace any organization in the county. Rather its chief objective is to coordinate and strengthen those agencies already in operation. It seeks to render a much needed religious emphasis to its acts of coordination.

"As was made crystal clear in the prospectus of organization, the Prince Edward Christian Association is governed by a constitution which defines its area of operation. The executive control of Prince Edward County Christian Association is vested in a president, two vice-presidents, a secretary, an assistant secretary, a treasurer, and an executive committee. The executive committee is composed of the officers and four lay members."

"The Constitution provides the following standing committees: Program Publicity, Voter-registration, Culture and Education, Finance and Auditing.

"The Prince Edward County Christian Association is currently completing the personnel of the above named committees. Meanwhile, the Executive Committee as a whole is currently conducting the bulk of the work. The overall objectives can be stated thusly:

1. To work toward the restoration of public schools in Prince Edward County.
2. To assist in corralling the necessary manpower and leadership of Prince Edward to assist in an all out poll tax, registration and voter campaign.
     a. This effort will embrace the active participation of both the youth and adult citizenry.
3. To coordinate the efforts on a county-wide basis of those organizations, groups and individuals (especially the NAACP) interested in restoring public education in Prince Edward County.
4.

The Association's immediate and crisis objective may be summarized thusly:

1. To initiate and supervise the placement of the Negro junior and senior high school students in accredited institutions of learning.
2. To set up study-play groups for the remaining children affected, lending such groups the necessary supervision and guidance.

3. To conduct a continuing educational and cultural program designed to elevate and broaden the cultural and educational perspective of the citizens of Prince Edward County and particularly the citizens of color.' "[58]

---

[58] Source: *The Prince Edward County Christian Association*—Writer: Reverend Dr. L. Francis Griffin, Sr.-1916-1980

The African Methodist Episcopal Church (AME)

*"God our Father, Christ our Redeemer, The Holy Spirit our
Comforter,
Humankind our Family."*
Founded: 1816

In maintaining the legacy for which it was founded, the African Methodist Episcopal Church (AME) was founded in protest against segregation and discrimination by Reverends Richard Allen (1760-1831); Absalom Jones (1746-1818); and Daniel Coker (1780-1846).

Reverends Allen and Jones founded the Free African Society (FAS), in 1787 for the primary purposes of satisfying and ministering to the needs of the sick, the unemployed, the widows, and the orphans. Their function was similar to that of The Loving Sisters of Worship and the True Reformers as stated in Part One of this book.

Allen, founder of Mother Bethel African Methodist Episcopal (AME) Church in Philadelphia, Pennsylvania in 1799, became an activist, orator, writer and Bishop. Mother Bethel is the longest continuously held piece of property by Black people in the United States. Harriett Tubman (1822-1913), the Chief Conductor (**God, the Engineer**) of the Underground Railroad was granted permission to use this "Church House" as a station to rest, recuperate, pray, collect and distribute ideas. Thus, Mother Bethel was a refuge from the tempest and a shelter in time of storm. She was a wayfarer's lodging for all her tired sojourning blood!

The AME Denomination had thought of itself as being the oldest Black denomination in the Nation. However, the establishment of the African Baptist Church in Silver Bluff, South Carolina under the leadership of George Liele and later Andrew Bryan in Savannah, Georgia in 1822 and respectively also of Mecklenburg County, Virginia; The First Baptist Church of Williamsburg, Virginia (1776) and The First Baptist Church of Petersburg, Virginia (1774) lay claim on being "**Firsts**."

Throughout its history, The AME's have had a total of more than thirty bishops. Of this amount three are women: Vashti Murphy

McKenzie (born 1937); Carolyn Tyler Guidry (born 1937); and Susan Frances Davis. In accordance with my observations, Henry McNeil Turner (1834-1915), is the leading torch bearer for all bishops in the areas of race relations and in general, social justice. Many colleges and Universities were named after several bishops.

The Beulah AME Church

In continuing its traditional racial stance in its struggle for Blacks, The Beulah Church's strongest role and most timely contributions to the movement was opening doors to Knowledge through Kittrell College for students who were denied educational advantages from 1959-1964. Their participation in street demonstrations during the summer of 1963, when several of us were jailed, brought relevancy to the community. Its pastor at that time, Reverend Goodwin Douglass, stated to me in a 2009 interview: "Each church had it own atmosphere."

Since the early 1940's, this church's educational contributions was the establishment of The Farmville Reading Room within the confines of its basement. In this particular undertaking, it stood unique in relation to other Black churches.

It was constructed in 1868 by all Blacks, who made the bricks while the sisters made nutritious meal preparations and other work. Historically, its membership composition consists of professionals and blue collar workers. The county's first Black Attorney, James Edward Ghee, is a life-long member of this congregation.

Kittrell College

Founded: 1886

The African Methodist Episcopal Church (AME) has claimed ownership of colleges and universities. They are as follows: Allen University 1870; Campbell College; Daniel Payne College 1889-1979; Edward Waters College 1866; Kittrell College 1886; Morris Brown 1881; Paul Quinn 1872; Payne Theological Seminary 1844; Shorter College 1816; Turner Theological Seminary 1894; and Wilberforce University 1865.

In the County of Prince Edward, Kittrell radiates more of a unique position than others. This is because of two factors: 1) its geographical location ninety miles from Farmville; and 2) Reverend A. I. Dunlap, Pastor at that time of the Beulah (AME) Church in Farmville and former teacher at the college and the Reverend Goodwin Douglass also former pastor of Beulah and an alumnus of Kittrell. Dunlap and Douglass pastured during the 1960's.

Dunlap was initially responsible for the planting of the seed of growth for students who were without schooling (1959-1964). Douglas resumed his work in this domain and Reverend Leslie Francis Griffin, Sr. was chief organizer of this ministry. Toward the end, Kittrell awarded Griffin an honorary Doctor of Divinity Degree.

Much of the work is outlined and written in the Prince Edward County Christian Association's plan and purposes, their goals, aims and objectives, as has been alluded.

This writer was an undergrad student at Shaw University in Raleigh, North Carolina during the formation of this virtuous and indigenous group, and upon coming home one weekend, Griffin remarked, "We are putting together an organization similar to that of King's Southern Christian Leadership Conference (SCLC)." I volunteered as one who would assist in voter registration drives during the time I was home for holidays and through the summer months.

Sixty-one students without schooling were sent to Kittrell Jr. College under the auspices of the Prince Edward County Christian Association (PECCA).

Singing the Lord's Songs in an Exiled Land

Singing was one phase of the struggle that formed a centerpiece of the movement. Transferring many songs from church to the movement gave us momentum, knowledge, religion and spiritual innovations and other resources that moved the movement and charged the cause![59]

During the sizzlin' sixties, the fervent cry throughout the land was **FREEDOM NOW!** This was not limited to street demonstrations, wade-in, sit-ins, etcetera, but to a broad-based amalgamation of other facets of the movement blended. We were re-introduced to Black Art and other humanities of our people who were committed architects of the Harlem Renaissance (1920's & 30's). Their theatrics, poetry and musical contributions were expression of their indigenous African genius!

From December 1, 1955 (Montgomery Bus Boycott began) throughout the inter-decades of the 60's and 70's, there was a great gear shifting in mobilization, radicalization and revolutionizing from the churches downward through the federal government and all structures of survival.

Many churches became liberalized and more relevant in their theological approaches to social problems. For example, The Second Vatican Council burst forth in the Catholic Church under the leadership of Pope John, the 23rd. The scholarly emphasis on the "Black Church" and "Black Theology" emerged as a dynamic response to "Black Power", an expression of Reverend Adam Clayton Powell, Jr., Pastor of New York's Abyssinian Baptist Church in Harlem; later spoken of by Willie Ricks of The Student Non-Violent Coordinating Committee (SNCC); and Stokley Carmichael Kwame Ture (1941-1998).

---

[59]   Michele Norman, Ph.D. Associate Professor of Communication Sciences and Disorders Longwood University

The writings of James Baldwin, Amiri Baraka (1934—LeRoi Jones); Nikki Giovanni (1943); Tony Morrison (1931); W.E.B. Dubois; Langston Hughes (1902-1967); Richard "Dick" Gregory (1932—); and scores of others saturated the atmosphere.

Then in similar fashion; singing, humming and moaning songs kept both Blacks and Whites in a state of exalted exuberance. The choosing of church hymns and church related hymns brought from God a kind of double deliverance: We were being delivered from oppression through His sustaining power; and the Black Church was the motivating source form which this spiritual joy triumphed.

Some of the following Negro Spirituals provided a just order for all occasions: **Go Down Moses, Jacob's Ladder, Didn't My Lord Deliver Daniel?, Steal Away**, and **Wade in the Water**. And there were church hymns slightly re-worded and rendered in a social justice context: **We Shall Overcome**,—taken from the Church hymn, **I'll Be Alright Someday**; **Woke up this morning with my mind stayed on Freedom**, from the hymn **Woke up this morning with my mind on Jesus; Ain't Gonna Let Nobody Turn Me Round; Guide my Feet Lord while I run this Race; Oh Freedom, and Kum-ba-ya, from the hymn, Come by here my Lord, Come by here.**

"If you listen to what Black people are singing religiously, it is a clue to what is happening to them sociologically."[60] These were among the basic "shouts" that were among other "moving forward" hymns. One could not sing them and feel non-spirit filled. They were stimulating literary words, set to music to give unity and cohesiveness to our toils, tragedies and triumphs.

Finally, in addition to the poetry writers and hymns, musicians joined the freedom march. Odetta Holmes (1930-2008), and Mahalia Jackson (1911-1972), were two vocalists, among others, who sang at the Mighty March on Washington, D.C. on August 28, 1963. Others that were present were James Brown (1933-2006); Harry Belafonte (1927-); Nina Simone (1933-2003); Aretha Franklin (1942-); Ray Charles (1935-2004); Stevie Wonder (1950-); Miriam Makeba (1932-2008); Hugh Masekela (1939-);.and Sam Cooke singing the Protest hymn: **A change gonna come.**

---

60   Wyatt Tee Walker-*The Soul of Black Worship, A Trilogy of Preaching, Praying, Singing*

The music, and or singing produced a powerful satisfying solace and assurance of hope to the movement. The Black Churches and many liberal whites became more activated when protest songs were brought "in" and street demonstration songs became more spiritualized when they were brought "out". It was a kind of antiphonal reciprocity with sweet synchronization!

Gerald W. Dees, M.D. sums up this section by writing: "*Music is universal and is found in every culture in the world. Music conveys social conditions, political thoughts, spiritual reflections and love. In other words music defines* <u>what's</u> *in our hearts, minds and souls.*"[61]

---

61   Source: *The New York Amsterdam News.*-February 3-9, 2011. Health Care: Face the Music

Toward Defining the Black Church in the Perceptive

Visions of its Clergypersons and Other Scholars
A Brief Historical Synopsis

Enforced laws of segregation and discrimination in social, economic, religious, academic and other spheres; have driven Black people into a state of exilic existence, physically, emotionally and psychologically! Grave contradictions have arisen between these laws on the federal, state and local levels. For instance, the Reconstruction Amendments: 13th, 14 th, and 15 th were counteracted by Jim Crow Laws 1876-1965; Black Codes; Ku Klux Klan in 1915; and the infamous State Rights components. We note in passing that the above Amendments pertained to abolishing slavery, producing voting rights and guaranteeing citizenship, respectively.

Dark and dismal have been the way of our sojourn. "Stony the road we trod, bitter the chastening rod," wrote James Weldon Johnson in our collective and solitary hymn: *Lift Every Voice and Sing.* But the Black Church enabled us to traverse our way through the labyrinth of slavery with total reliance upon the "God of our weary years!"

In its crucible we have been molded, shaped and sent on our way to conquer and achieve in every vestige of living, it has been our hope and sustenance for both church and non-attendees.

The Black Church has always been a spiritually active conglomerate, having been birthed from the womb of protest, revolt and recalcitrance against the evils of inhumane treatment inherent in a culture of white supremacy and a so-called democracy. With this thought in mind, Henry H. Mitchell, one of the most prolific writers of Black Theology and Ecclesiastical History of our church, writes: " . . . at its best, the African American church has proven to be the greatest source for motivating self-liberation action, as well as healthy self-pride among African Americans. In addition, no other aspect or agency of the common cultures comes close to the Vanguard of African American churches in retention of African influences on Black Culture."[62] Take notice that Mitchell's grandfather, Henry H. Mitchell was the second pastor of the aforementioned First Baptist Church.

Among the earliest protestors of the Black Church were Richard Allen (1740-1831); Absolom Jones (1746-1818); and Daniel Coker (1780-1846). These and other Black worshippers were snatched from their feet while praying in a gallery (reserved for slaves), in The St. George's Methodist Episcopal Church in Philadelphia, Pennsylvania in 1787. From out of this protest, the African Methodist Episcopal Church was given birth. Daniel Coker was offered the bishopric as its first appointee however he declined the position. Allen then attained this post and proceeded to organize the AME Church in 1816. And, following this action Allen and Jones succeeded in organizing The Free African Society, a mutual aid society in the same context of the True Reformers, aforementioned.

Allen could have named the first Black Methodist denomination: "American," but "African" was more appropriate because of its historical resource and meaningfulness.

Chattel slavery was defeated not primarily because of the Constitution, its Thirteenth, fourteenth and Fifteenth Amendments, or Abraham Lincoln's Emancipation Proclamation signed, January 1, 1863, in mid-Civil War (1861-1865), but through the delivery and liberating effect of the Black Preacher, his congregants and other church-related organizations. We wrestled the negative and inhumane prejudice of slavery and "beat the white man at his own game," once stated to me by a former classmate in Virginia Union's School of Religion, now the illustrious President and alumnus of Lynchburg's (VA) oldest college, Virginia University, Dr. Ralph Reavis. Both schools have adopted name changes since their inception.

From home to church, to school and community, Black folk have always been adept and relevant in converting the negatives

---

[62] Source: *Black Church Beginnings: The Long Hidden Realities of the First Years,*-William B. Erdmans Publishing Company, Grand Rapids, Michigan/Cambridge, United Kingdom

of a white racist society into positive effects. In the sizzlin' 60's we referred to this as being, "getting over on the man," or "techniques of survival in the Black Community!" We are a transcending race. From whence did this emerge? From the depth of our soul's African indigenousness!

Africa, the home of all World cultures, races and ethnicities! Now hear ye them!

1. *"The Black Church is the American fruit of an African root."*[63]

2. It is generally agreed that the Negro Church is the greatest institution developed by Negroes than any other organization, and it has more influence in molding the thoughts and life of Negro people than any other simple agency.[64]

3. The Black Church was never devoted to war. Bloody Violence is a topic rarely associated with the Black Church. Nevertheless, the three best-known violent slave insurrections had strong religious basis. These bear closer examination: The Gabriel Processor Conspiracy, 1800; The Denmark Vessey rebellion, 1882; and the Nat Turner insurrection, 1831.[65]

4. In their struggle against racism, Black Churches have never understood themselves as a narrow self-interest group seeking only their satisfaction. On the contrary, they have sought to save the republic from self-destruction of the malignant racism that threatens the well-being of the nation.[66]

---

[63] Wyatt Tee Walker: Theologian, Author, Cultural Historian, and former Chief of Staff to Martin Luther King, Jr.

[64] Source: *Dark Glory*—Harry V. Richardson, Friendship Press-New York

[65] Source: *Black Church Beginnings: The Long Hidden Realities of The First Years,* Henry H. Mitchell

[66] Ibid

5. The Black Pilgrimage to America was made less onerous because of their religion. Their religion was the organizing principle around which their life was structured. Their church was their school, their forum, their political arena, their social club, their art gallery, and their conservatory of music. It was lyceum and gymnasium as well as sanctum sanctorum. Their religion was the peculiar sustaining force that gave them the strength to endure when endurance gave no promise, and the courage to be creative in the face of their own dehumanization.[67]

6. By thinking Black and acting colorlessly, the Black Church continues to bring hope and inspiration to Black people. The institutional and personal racism with which Black Americans have struggled is discouraging and dehumanizing. The Black Church, by thinking Black and acting colorlessly, has the power to equip Black people to survive and thrive. Further, thinking Black and acting colorlessly enables The Black Church to engage effectively in global missions.[68]

7. In writing from the vantage point of an insider, *John Mercer Langston,* praised the Negro Church for giving to "**Colored Americans**" the opportunity to be himself, to think his own thoughts, to express his own convictions, to make his own utterances, test his own power and thus, and in the exercises of the faculties of his own soul, trust and achieve.[69]

---

[67] Sources: *The Black Church in the African American Experience.*-C. Eric Lincoln and Lawrence H. Mamiya (p.93) as copied from Lincoln's and Gayraud Wilmore's work: *Black Religion and Black Radicalism: An Interpretation of the Religious History of African Americans (p.7)*

[68] Source: *A Divine assignment: The Missiology of Wendell Clay Somerville.*—David Emmanuel Goatley (p.42)

[69] Source: *John Mercer Langston-(1829-1897),U. S. public official, diplomat, educator, attorney, and political activist*

8. Especially in the Nineteenth and early Twentieth Century's, Black Churches generated extensive programs as part of the larger philosophy of radical self-help. In response to a hostile environment that denied so many opportunities and services to the Black Community Black Churches nurtured schools, health clinics, publishing houses, libraries, recreation centers, and innumerable other organizations. In his commencement address to the Class of 1898 at Fisk University, *W.E.B. Dubois;* stated that Black Churches were *'for the most part, curiously composite institutions, which combine the work of churches, theaters, newspapers, homes, schools and lodges.'*[70]

9. The Black Church is a *"Nation within a Nation."*[71]

10. The most highly developed and characteristic expression of Negro life . . . . as throughout the Union is the Negro Church. The church is, among American Negroes, the primitive social group of slaves on American soil, replacing the tribal life roughly disorganized by the slave ship, and in many respects antedating the establishing of the Negro monogamist home. The church is much more than a religious organization; it is the chief organ of social intellectual discourse.[72]

11. The Black Church obviously began as a spiritual sanctuary and community against a violent and destructive character of the slave world . . . It served as an agency of social reorientation and reconstruction, providing reinforcements for the old values of marriage, family, morality and spirituality in the face of corrosive effects of slavery . . . . The church became the center for economic cooperation, pooling resources to buy church buildings, mutual aid

---

[70] Source: *Righteous Discontent: The Women's Movement in the Black Baptist Church, 1880-1920.* Evelyn Brooks Higginbotham

[71] Source: E. Franklin Frazier

[72] Source: William Edward Burghardt DuBois, Ph.D.

societies which provided social services for free Blacks and helping re-slaved Africans by purchasing and setting up businesses for economic development . . . . The church engaged in both public and internal projects, setting up schools, training ministers, teachers and raising funds to carry on these projects . . . . The Black Church from its earliest days as an invisible spiritual community, supported social change, providing readers and leadership at various points in the struggle for Black liberation and a truly higher level of human life.[73]

12. The Black Preacher is the most unique personality developed by the Negro on American soil.[74]

13. The Black Church has been the backbone of the Black community. First Baptist ministers preached liberal theology emphasizing "social action without regard of race or creed." It has always been the location for community meetings, especially social action agendas. The Black Church is noted for its fiery preaching, beautiful music from slave songs to contemporary music, as well as scriptural anthems.[75]

14. The Black Church—a piece of the fabric of society.

My perceptions of the Black Church are based on 45 plus years of active membership in the Black Baptist Church and research that I have conducted for diverse academic topics relating to the black family. The Black Church is one of the strongest and one of the most fundamental social institutions in society. It is here that the blueprint provides

---

[73] Source: *Introduction to Black Studies,* Mulana Karenga, Ph.D.—Father of Kwanza in America, Scholar, Author and Lecturer

[74] Source: William Edward Burghardt DuBois, Ph.D.

[75] Source: Edna Allen Dean, Ph.D.; Professor Emerita of Longwood University

the mechanisms for the survival and growth of the black family.[76]

15. The Black Church is an intrinsic, inspired articulation of spiritual freedom in Christ Jesus; sharing life, love and care for God's people.[77]

16. Historically, The Black Church has been a core institution for African American philanthropy. The Black Church does not serve as a faith-based house of Worship, but it facilitates organized philanthropic efforts including meeting spiritual, psychological, financial, educational and basic humanitarian such as food, housing, and shelter needs. Black Churches are, also involved in organizing and providing volunteers to the community and in Civil and human rights activism. Most Black Churches are community focused . . . . Philanthropy, and The Black Church also provided moral, spiritual and political leadership.[78]

17. The ache for home lives in all of us, the safe place we can go as we are and not be questioned.[79]

---

[76] Source: Theresa A. Clark, Ph.D.; Department Chair, Associate Professor of Social Work and Area Coordinator of Longwood University

[77] Pastor Lisa Terry; Kingdom Community Church, Crewe, Virginia

[78] Source: Latasha Chaffin—Graduate student—Grand Valley State University

[79] Source: Maya Angelou (1928-)

A Prayer Written and Prayed

by

J. Samuel Williams, Jr., '52

Pastor

The Levi Baptist Church

Green Bay, Virginia

National Historic Landmark Ceremony

August 31, 1998

Board Member Robert R. Moton Museum

The Prayer

Beneath the canopy of your sky, upon these hallowed grounds and amid those of us who have taken history seriously, O God, the Transcender of time and space, we humbly acknowledge your Omnipresence among us this August day on such an august occasion!

For this great gathering of your sons, daughters, alumni, alumnae, family and friends, in the serenity of this moment of grandeur, we have come in expression of our human gratitude for such a Divine Reality.

Thanks to you for those indwelling and penetrating spirits, for the unswerving and committed deeds of Robert Russa Moton, Martha E. Forrester (and her present sons and daughters), Barbara Johns, Vernon Napoleon Johns, Leslie Francis Griffin, Sr. For these are they whom you sent to toil in the wilderness, thereby constructing and instructing in us the knowledge, skills and bravery in diverse but unified ways, to combine courage with vision amid racial adversity, indifference and exploitation.

Be thou gracious to parents, grandparents and other kindred for their zeal and fortitude to fight against racial bigotry, prejudice and ignorance, as well as those whose spirits abide with you eternally, whose bodies are resting in the earth from which they were drawn.

Consecrate the work of this future museum so that peoples of all races, religious preferences, social ideologies, political philosophies and persuasions may come to seek, to search and to save humankind, as we, with great diligence, awe and expectations, burst forth into the new millennium.

May each of us return to our homes and hamlets, villages and cities to begin to rid ourselves of the differences which we have caused, and to study racial war, no more!

You are the "God of our weary years, God of our silent tears;" "God of our Fathers who's Almighty Hand" the God of Abraham, Isaac and Jacob and their wives Sarah, Rebecca, Leah, and Rachel.

Amen

Reliable Resources

(Bibliography)

Boyle, Sarah Patton—*The Desegregated Heart*

Burrell, Charles E.—*History of Prince Edward County*

Burrell, Charles E.—*History of Prince Edward County, Virginia*

Cleage, Albert—*The Black Messiah*

Cone, James—*Black Theology and Black Power*

Cone, James—*For My People: Black Theology and The Black Church*

Cone, James—*God of the Oppressed*

Felder, Cain Hope—*Troubling Biblical Waters: Race, Class, and Family*

Fisher, Miles Mark—*Negro Slave songs in the United States*

Foster, Vonita W.—*Silent Trumpets of Justice*

Franklin, John Hope—*From Slavery to Freedom*

Frazier, E. Franklin—*The Black Church in America*

George, Carol R. V.—*Segregated Sabbaths*

Harris, James Henry—*Practicing Liberation Theology in the Black Church*

In Religion.

Hicks, Terrance and Abul Pitre—*The Educational Lockout of African Americans in*

Prince Edward County, Virginia (1959-1964). Personal Accounts and Reflections edited by:

Jackson, Jr., Kennell—*America is Me*

James, George G.M.—*Stolen Legacy*

King, Jr., Martin Luther—*Stride Toward Freedom*

King, Jr., Martin Luther—*Where Do We Go From Here? Chaos or Community*

Kluger, Richard—*Simple Justice*

Lincoln, C. Eric and L.H. Mamiya—*The Black Church in the African American*

Experience

Lincoln, C. Eric—*The Black Church since Frazier*

Lincoln, C. Eric—*The Black Muslim in America*

Marsh, Clifton E.—*From Black Muslims to Muslims: The Resurrection Transformation and Change of the Lost Found Nation of Islam in America 1930-1995*

Martin, Sandy D.—*Black Baptist and African Missions*

Mays, Benjamin E. and Joseph W. Nicholson—*The Negro Church*

Mays, Benjamin Elijah—*The Negro's God as Reflected in his Literature*

McGraw, Marie Tyler—*Black and Whites in the making of Liberia: An African Republic*

Myrdal, Gunnar—*An American Dilemma*

Powell, Henry—*Remembering Vernon Johns*

Rabateau, Albert J.—*Slave Religion*

Roberts, J. Deotis—*Black Theology: Liberation and Contextualization*

Smith, Bob—*They Closed Their Schools*

Stokes, John—*Students on Strike: Jim Crow, Civil Rights and Me*

Sullivan, Neil V.—*Bound For Freedom*

Thurman, Howard—*The Luminous Darkness*

Thurman, Howard—*Jesus and the Disinherited*

Thurman, Howard—*The Desegregated Heart* van Sertima, Ivan—*They Came Before Columbus*

Walker, Wyatt Tee—*Somebody's Calling My Name*

Wall, William B.—*History of Farmville, Virginia 1798-1948, The Farmville Herald*

Washington, Jr., Joseph R.—*Black Religion*

Washington, Jr., Joseph R—*Black Sects and Cults*

Wilmore, Gayraud S.—*Black Religion and Black Radicalism*

Woodson, Carter G.—*The History of the Negro Church*

The Moving Finger writes;

and having writ,

moves on: Nor all your piety nor wit

shall lure it back to cancel half a line

nor all you tears wash out a word of it.

The Rubaiyat of Omar Khayyam (1048-1131)

www.ingramcontent.com/pod-product-compliance
Lightning Source LLC
Chambersburg PA
CBHW031235280526
45784CB00004B/1589